Six Records of a Floating Life

Shen Fu

Translated by Alex Fang

Printim Editions

First Published in 2025 by Printim Editions

Printed and bound by TJ Books 2025

ISBN – 979-8-9874792-5-4

Copyright © Printim Editions 2025

The right of Alex Fang to be identified as the owner of this translation has been asserted by her in accordance with the Copyright, Designs and Patents Act 1988

All rights reserved. No part of this publication may be reproduced, stored in a retrieval system, or transmitted, in any form, or by any means (electronic, mechanical, photocopying, recording or otherwise) without the permission of the publisher.

Translated from Classical Chinese into English by Alex Fang

First Edition

Originally published as 浮生六記

228 Park Avenue S.
New York, NY 10003
www.printimeditions.com

For Nick

Translator's Preface

Few things delighted Chen Yun, the love of Shen Fu's life and the soul of this book, more than the chance discovery of fragmented manuscripts, which she would then bind with care. It is thus fitting that *Six Records of a Floating Life* was published only posthumously, in 1877, after being found in manuscript form at an inconspicuous book stand in Shen's native Suzhou, with only the first four of its six intended records surviving. This is also to say that, like the life of its author, *Six Records* drifted.

The historical person of Shen has remained obscure. Most of what we know of him comes from this autobiography alone: that he was born in 1763 to a scholarly family, married Chen in 1780 after the two fell in love as children, and held a series of low-level bureaucratic posts, working between them as an art dealer and, briefly, a merchant. The span of Shen's experience means that his personal narrative also doubles as an unguarded window into life and society in late imperial China, framed by the civil service examination system, patrilineal kinship structure, regional and foreign trade, as well as prevalent practices of Buddhism, Taoism, and folk religion.

As a character, Shen is fallible, and he was aware of his foibles. One wonders if this awareness was what gave rise to the autobiography its nonlinear, quasi-palimpsestic construction: *Six Records* unfolds in thematic chapters that are each largely self-contained and internally chronological, yet speak to and refract upon one another. The first record tells of a love story that is almost an idyll, but ends abruptly at the first stirring of grief. The second record, at times veering toward a connoisseur's manual, details the couple's various idle pleasures and aesthetic pursuits, perhaps a kind of self-soothing that readies the writer for the self-lacerating confessions soon to follow. In the third chapter, we witness the distress and calamities the couple endured in those very same years and the bitter circumstances surrounding Chen's death, for which Shen offers himself up as culpable. From there the book begins to quite literally wander, as Shen recounts his travels through Qing China, from which Chen was mostly excluded as a matter of social norms. The effect is such that, even though Chen is alive during the temporal frame of this final record, her absence haunts throughout.

Something beautiful was once had and is now lost. The poet cannot help but look back, aware that what remains is only the poem, not the person. The reader, however, is gifted this moving narrative—itself almost lost once more but here with us by some grace or accident. And perhaps more than that, the reader is granted a glimpse of inner freedom. To the extent the third chapter, "Record of Trying Sorrow," inflects the second, "Record of Idle Pleasures," the inverse is just as true: we see a couple who, even at their most destitute, held fast to ideals of beauty and love. *Six Records* is also a rarity among classical Chinese texts in its portrayal of what the contemporary reader might recognize as a polyamorous liaison, borne out of sapphic desire—striking, given the patriarchal era Chen lived in. By Shen's own account, the couple paid dearly for their defiance. Yet it is this very entwinement of pleasure and pain, of freedom and frustration, that renders their shared life enduring—relived each time it is read, worthy of return not in spite of its sorrow but because of all that made it whole.

Alex Fang
June 2025

RECORD OF DOMESTIC JOY

I was born in the winter of Gui Wei during the reign of Emperor Qianlong,[1] on the twenty-second day of the eleventh month.[2] The country was in its heyday of peace and prosperity, and I was raised in a scholar-official family residing by the Pavilion of Azure Waves in Suzhou. It could thus be said that the heavens had been remarkably kind to me.

There is the Dongpo[3] line that goes, "Past affairs evanesce, like spring dreams without a trace." Should I not record mine with my inkbrush, I am afraid it would be a squandering of the great blue's favors to me.

Considering, out of its three hundred, *The Classic of Poetry*[4] begins with one on courtship, I shall begin my volume with a chapter on wedded love and let the rest follow. I do regret that I was far from studious in my younger years and thus cannot profess to be well-lettered. All I can do is document sentiments as real as the events themselves. If one were to scrutinize the merits of my writing in terms of composition, that would be like expecting gloss from a tarnished mirror.

I was betrothed in my childhood to a Miss Yu of Jinsha, who died at eight years of age. I subsequently married Miss Chen, given name Yun, courtesy name[5] Shuzhen, the daughter of my maternal uncle Xinyu. She was nimble-witted even as a young girl when she was just

---

[1]. Year 1763, in the Qing dynasty (1644–1912). Gui and Wei are, respectively, tenth and eighth of the heavenly stems and earthly branches, the latter part of a system involving a sexagenary cycle used to record years.

[2]. All references to months are according to the Chinese lunisolar calendar.

[3]. Su Shi (1037–1101), one of the most prominent writers of the Song dynasty.

[4]. *The Classic of Poetry: Shijing*, the oldest surviving collection of Chinese poetry dating from the 11th to 6th century BCE (Western Zhou dynasty to the Spring and Autumn period)

[5]. A courtesy name, also known as a style name, is an additional name given to a person upon adulthood as a complement to their given name.

learning to speak. She was able to recite "Ballad of the Lute" just by hearing it read to her.

At four years of age, she lost her father and was left with only her mother, Madam Jin, and brother, Kechang, in a household destitute of possessions within its bare walls. As Yun grew up, she became quite adept at needlework. The family of three depended on the workings of her ten fingers for provisions, and she made certain that Kechang never missed a single payment for tuition.

One day, she got hold of a copy of "Ballad of the Lute" from her brother's book basket and learned to read word by word. Between intervals of her work in embroidery, she versed herself in poetry and rhetoric over time, and composed such clever lines as

Autumn-scathed, the human figure wanes.
Frost-cast, the chrysanthemum thickens.

When I was thirteen years old, I went with my mother to her maiden home, and there Yun and I became inseparable. I had the chance to see her poems, and though I admired her brilliance, I was already seized by a private apprehension then that she might not be equally blessed in her fortune.

She hence stayed on my mind persistently. I said to my mother, "If you were to choose a wife for me, it would have to be cousin Shu, or I would refuse to marry." My mother, who also loved Yun's gentle temperament, was quick to arrange our union and bestowed on Yun the gold ring from her own finger. This was the sixteenth day of the seventh month, in the year of Yi Mo.[6]

---

6. 1775.

In the middle of that winter, another cousin on my mother's side was to become a bride, and I accompanied my mother again to visit her family. Yun and I were of the same year, her being ten months older. We had always called each other "big sister" and "little brother" from childhood, and so I continued to address her as "Sister Shu."

On this festive occasion, the room was overflowing with bright-colored garments, with Yun alone dressed plainly in quiet colors; only her pair of shoes were new. I saw that they were finely embroidered, and learned upon my inquiry that she had crafted the shoes herself. Only then did I realize her gifts were not confined to the literary.

With sloped shoulders and a long neck, she had a slender, but not bony, figure. Her brows were finely arched and her gracefully shaped eyes shone with intelligence and vitality. Only her two front teeth—and one could perhaps call this a blemish—were slightly protruding. Yet there was an air of tenderness about her that seemed capable of wearing away all evils in one's heart.

I asked for her manuscripts of poems and saw that many of them consisted only of a couplet, or else just three, four lines; few were complete. I inquired as to the reason. She replied with a chuckle, "These were composed without proper instruction. If only I had a dear teacher and bosom friend to help me refine and finish these lines!"

I inscribed on the cover of her manuscript, "Brocade Pouch of Fine Verses," in good humor, not knowing her untimely death had been portended thence.[7]

That night, we escorted the bride outside the city, and by the time we returned, it was already the small hours of morning. I was quite starved and asked for a snack. The maid brought some dried dates, but I found them much too sweet. Furtively Yun pulled me into her room by the sleeve, and I saw that she had stashed some warm congee and sides.

---

7. Likely a reference back to the lines, "Autumn-scathed, the human figure wanes. / Frost-cast, the chrysanthemum thickens." Chrysanthemums are associated with funerals.

Just as I picked up my chopsticks gleefully, we heard Yun's cousin Yuheng call out, "Sister Shu, come quick!" At this Yun hurried to shut the door, "I am all tired out and going to bed." But Yuheng managed to shove himself in, seeing that I was about to eat the congee, and remarked to Yun with a grin, "When I asked you for congee, you said it was all gone. I see now that you were hiding it away for your future husband!"

Yun was greatly embarrassed and thus excused herself, while everybody out in the courtyard was laughing. I felt vexed as well and went home early with my old servant.

Having been ridiculed for this congee affair, Yun avoided me whenever I visited. I knew, however, that she was simply wary of once more being made a laughingstock.

Thenceforth came our wedding night, on the twenty-second day of the first month in the year of Geng Zi. I saw that her figure was as thin and frail as before. Her veil having been lifted, we gazed into each other's eyes and smiled. After crossing our nuptial wine cups, we sat down side by side for dinner. Under the table, I secretly held her hand—so delicate, warm, and smooth, in mine—and in my chest my heart was beating uncontrollably.

I prompted her to eat but learned that she was in her days of vegetarian observance,[8] which she had been practicing for several years. I reckoned that she had started such observance around the same time of my chickenpox outbreak and so said with a chuckle, "Well, now that I am smooth-skinned and without ailments, dear sister, will you finally break your observance?" She looked at me with smiling eyes and nodded.

My own sister was to wed on the twenty-fourth, and on the twenty-third the country was to be in mourning,[9] so we had a

---

8. Practiced by Chinese Buddhists.
9. Day to mourn for the death of the emperor or empress consort, on which music and celebrations were not allowed.

farewell banquet for our sister on the twenty-second instead, with Yun attending with me. I was playing the finger guessing drinking game with the bridesmaid in our own wedding chamber, but lost to her almost in every round and passed out completely drunk. By the time I woke up, Yun was already in the midst of her morning toilette.

The day bustled with the arrival of friends and family, and the celebrations commenced promptly once the evening lights came on. At midnight on the twenty-fourth, I sent off the bride as the new brother-in-law, and when I returned close to three o'clock, all the lights had faded in the quiet of the night.

I tiptoed into the room to see that the bridesmaid was sound asleep under the bed, but that Yun, having removed her makeup, was still up. She had a fine candle lit and was reading with her head down, her rosy neck exposed. I wondered what book got her so completely absorbed.

"Dear sister, you've had such a long day, why so tirelessly studious still?" I said, giving her a gentle pat on the shoulder.

Turning around hastily, Yun stood up and answered, "I was just about to go to bed, but I opened the cabinet and found this book. As I started reading it, I came to forget all the fatigue. I had heard of *Romance of the Western Chamber* for a while now but only saw it for the first time today. It is truly a work of genius, only I find the style rather acerbic."

"Only a genius can write so acerbically," I said with a laugh.

The bridesmaid urged us to go to bed, and I told her to retire first and leave the door shut behind her. Yun and I then sat side by side and we joked together like close friends reuniting after a long separation.

I touched her chest tentatively to find that her heart was pounding, too. Bending over, I whispered into her ear, "Dear sister, why is your heart beating so fast like that?" Yun looked back at me with a smile, and I felt a thread of love and affection tugging my soul.

I pulled her into the canopy of the bed, and did not notice when the sky whitened in the east.[10]

樂

As a new wife, Yun was very quiet at first and never showed any anger. Whatever one said to her, she would only smile back in response. She treated those above her with reverence and those below her with kindness. She was well-organized and, indeed, faultless. Every morning she would rise briskly and get dressed as soon as the sun shone upon the window, as if someone had been hurrying her. I asked her in amusement, "Now that we are wedded, things are no longer as when we ate congee that night anymore. How come you are still so afraid of gossip?"

"I was made a subject of ridicule for hiding away the congee for you then. There is no fear of mockery now, but I am afraid that our parents might think the new wife a lazybones."

As much as I wanted her in bed with me for longer, I did respect her virtuousness, so I started to rise early with her as well. Since then, we always remained close and inseparable as a figure and its shadow. Our love and affection defied what can be put into words.

Time passes easily when one is in joy, as the first month of our married life did in the blink of an eye, and presently my father, Sir Jiafu, who was at the time in official service in Kuaiji,[11] sent someone for me to go back and resume my studies under the tutorship of Master Zhao Shengzhai of Wulin.[12]

Master Zhao was a fine teacher, and the fact I can write at all today was entirely to his credit. When I came home for the wedding, we had

---

10. Sky whitened in the east: an allusion to Su Shi's "Former Ode on the Red Cliffs," which is referenced again later in the text.
11. Now Shaoxing in the province of Zhejiang.
12. Now Hangzhou in the province of Zhejiang.

agreed that I would return to Master Zhao's immediately after. Yet upon reading the letter, I still felt quite glum and was afraid that Yun might break into tears in front of others. But Yun, on the other hand, managed to put on a smile, encouraged me to go, and packed up my things for me.

Something was different in her countenance that night, but only slightly. When it was time for me to depart, she whispered to me, "Take good care of yourself, for there will be no one to look after you."

I then boarded the boat, which was soon unfastened.

It was the season when peach and plum blossoms vied with each other for beauty, but I felt disoriented as a bird lost from its flock in the forest, not recognizing any of its surroundings. The moment I got to Master Zhao's place, my father left and crossed the river to the east.

I stayed there for three months, which felt like a decade. Though Yun occasionally sent letters, they always responded to only half my inquiries. Compounding my disappointment, half of her letters were merely words of encouragement, with the rest being pleasantries. Upon wind arising in the bamboo courtyard and the moon shining on my window behind the banana leaves, I would always be seized amidst such scenes by a passionate longing for her.

When Master Zhao somehow learned of this, he wrote to my father at once, saying he would compose ten questions for my examination and thereafter send me home for the time being.

I was overjoyed like a garrisoned soldier excused from his post, except once aboard the boat, I felt every second as if it were a year. After having finally arrived home and answered all my mother's inquiries, I went immediately into our chamber to see Yun rise to greet me. We held each other's hands without exchanging a word, and our souls liquefied into fine mists in an instant. My ears buzzed. I forgot where my body was.

It was the time of June, and the inner chamber was hot as a steamer. Fortunately, we lived right by the Lotus Lovers' Lodge, which was a part of the Pavilion of Azure Waves to our east. Inside the wooden corridor bridge, there was a veranda overlooking the creek named "I Take," after the meaning of "I shall take clear water to launder my tassel, muddy water to wash my feet."[13] Its eaves faced out to an old tree, which covered the window with a dense shade and cast a green light on all human faces thereunder. On the bank across from the veranda, an endless stream of sightseers moved to and fro. This was where my father, Sir Jiafu, would entertain dinner guests behind closed curtains.

On my mother's orders I brought Yun here to spend the summer. She paused her embroidery due to the heat and instead spent her entire days with me, reading books and discussing the antiquities, or else adoring the moon and remarking on the flowers. Yun was not much of a drinker but could take up to three cups if so compelled, and I also taught her the drinking game "shooting the hidden." I thought to myself that there was no greater joy on earth than this.

One day, Yun asked me: "Of all the classical texts, which would be the best to learn from?"

"*Stratagems of the States* and *The Nanhua*, for their agility and wit; Kuang Heng and Liu Xiang, for their elegance and vigor; Shi Qian and Ban Gu, for their erudition and breadth; the naturalness of Changli, the ruggedness of Liuzhou, the romanticism of Luling, the eloquence of the three Sus.[14]

---

13. From Mencius' *Li Lou*.
14. Here Shen often refers to the texts or writers by shorthand. *Stratagems of the States*: *Stratagems of the Warring States*, a collection of writings from the Warring States period (490–221 BCE), compiled by Western Han dynasty scholar, Liu Xiang (77–6 BCE); *The Nanhua: The Zhuangzi*, an eponymous anthology of Zhuangzi (literally, Master Zhuang; 4th century BCE), pivotal figure in classical philosophical daoism; Shi Qian: Sima Qian (c. 145–c. 86 BCE), Western Han dynasty historian; Changli: Han Yu (768–824), Tang dynasty poet, essayist, and scholar-official; Liuzhou: Liu Zongyuan (773–819), Tang dynasty poet and essayist; Luling: Ouyang Xiu (1007–1072), Song dynasty poet, historian, and politician; the Three Sus: Su Shi, his father Su Xun (1009–1066), and younger brother Su Zhe (1039–1112), all prominent writers of the Song dynasty.

"There are also the political essays of Jia and Dong, the parallel prose of Yu and Xu, the memoranda of Lu Zhi, and many other instructive writings, more than one can enumerate. It all depends on the reader's capacity for perception and apprehension.[15]

"The quality of classical writing all depends on intellectual rigor and stylistic vigor, and this I fear would be difficult for a woman to master," Yun replied. "Only in the matter of poetry can I say I have some limited understanding."

"In the Tang Dynasty, poetry was a subject of the official examinations, and Li and Du[16] were the utmost virtuosos without a doubt," I said. "Which poet would you learn from?"

"Du's poems are highly honed and refined," Yun opined. "Li's, on the other hand, are expressive and unrestrained. Rather than Du's austerity, I would much prefer to learn from Li's uninhibited freedom."

"The Ministry of Works[17] epitomizes the height of the art of poetry," I said, "Most poets emulate him, yet you alone prefer Li. Why is that?"

"Du is certainly unparalleled in terms of his tight regulation of verses and thoughtful development of theme," Yun answered. "But Li's poems have the ethereal appeal of a fairy on Mount Guye and delight like falling petals and flowing water. It is not that Du is inferior to Li, only that my own heart does not yearn for the guidance of Du but loves Li deeply."

I laughed and said, "I must say I did not expect Chen Shuzhen to be an alter ego of Li Qinglian!"[18]

---

15. Jia and Dong: Jia Yi (c. 200–169 BCE) and Dong Zhongshu (179–104 BCE), both of the Western Han dynasty; parallel prose: pianwen, a literary writing style characterized by antithetic construction and balanced tonal patterns without the use of rhyme; Yu and Xu: Yu Xin (513–581) of the Northern Zhou dynasty and Xu Ling (507–583) of the Southern Liang dynasty.
16. Li and Du: Li Bai (701–762) and Du Fu (712–770), whose names are all but synonymous with Tang poetry.
17. This refers to Du, who held a position in the Ministry of Works.
18. Here Shen refers to Li Bai by his literary name, after Li's hometown Qinglian, literally, blue lotus.

Yun laughed, too, and continued, "I also hold in my heart Master Bai Letian,[19] who first introduced me to the art of poetry. There my sentiment of gratitude has not dissipated even a little."

"Why do you say that?" I asked.

"Was he not the one who composed 'Ballad of the Lute'?" Yun said.

"How curious!" I laughed and said, "Li Taibai[20] is your alter ego, Bai Letian your first mentor, and your husband's courtesy name is Sanbai. How come you have such a fated connection with the character Bai?"

Yun laughed, too, and said, "Since I do have such a fated connection with the character Bai, I'm afraid my writing will be riddled with Bai characters to come." (In the Wu dialect,[21] we call miswritten characters "Bai characters.") At this we both laughed heartily.

"Since you understand poetry, do you also have a preference among the odes?" I asked.

"*The Chu Ci*[22] is the origin of odes, though I find it difficult to understand in my shallow study of it," Yun replied. "Among the Han and Jin writers, it seems to me that Xiangru[23] has the best odes in terms of their elevation of tone and concision of diction."

"Perhaps," I said, "Wenjun did not fall in love with Changqing[24] for his *guqin*[25] tunes but for precisely this?" We both laughed again in conclusion of this exchange.

---

19. Bai Juyi (772–846), Tang dynasty poet and politician.
20. Here Shen refers to Li Bai by his courtesy name.
21. Wu: Suzhou.
22. Anthology of lyric poems attributed primarily to Qu Yuan (342–278 BCE) and Song Yu (298–222 BCE), both from the State of Chu of the Warring States period.
23. Sima Xiangru (179–117 BCE), poet, historian and politician of the Western Han dynasty.
24. Courtesy name of Sima Xiangru.
25. A plucked string instrument.

I am by nature candid, carefree, and without constraints; Yun, on the other hand, conforms to convention and courtesies, almost like a Confucian scholar. When I would occasionally help her dress or adjust her sleeve, she would always say, "I beg your pardon." Or if I handed her so much as a handkerchief or fan, she would always stand up to accept it.

I detested this at first and said to her, "Are you trying to bind me with all this etiquette? As the saying goes, 'Excessive propriety belies deceit.'"

At this Yun's cheeks turned red.

"I am only trying to be respectful with my etiquette. How can you say I am deceitful?" she replied.

"Respect resides in the heart, not in empty formalities," I said.

"There is no relationship more intimate than the ones we have with our parents," she countered. "But can we only respect them in our hearts while acting presumptuously toward them?"

"Oh, I was only joking earlier!" I said.

"Much of the strife in the world begins with joking," Yun replied. "Pray don't make such accusations of me in the future. Or else I could die of frustration!"

Pulling her into my arms, I comforted her until she finally relaxed her countenance into a smile. From then on, expressions like "Dare I…" and "I beg your pardon" became regular articles in our exchanges. We maintained such respectful courtesy with each other for the next twenty-three years, and our affection toward each other only deepened with time.

Inside the house, whether running into each other in a dark room or in a narrow corridor, we would always reach out to hold each other's hands and ask, "Where are you going?" We did so with a kind of surreptitious caution, as if we feared others might see us.

As a matter of fact, we even avoided being seen sitting or walking together by others at first, but as time went on, we no longer paid it any mind. If Yun was conversing with others and saw me approaching, she would immediately stand up and move slightly aside, and I would sit next to her.

Neither of us did this without being conscious of it, and though we both felt sheepish about it initially, gradually we thought no more of it. I now find it strange when I see elderly couples who look at each other as if they were enemies—how could that be? Some say, "If not so, how could two people grow old together?" Could that really be true?

On that year's Double Seventh Night,[26] Yun had prepared some incense, candles, melons, and other fruits, with which we both paid homage to the celestial deity in the "I Take" veranda. I had carved two seals, one with the inscription *May we be husband and wife in every lifetime* in red for me, the other with the same inscribed in white for Yun, to be used in our future correspondence.

The moonlight was beautiful that night. Down in the river we saw ripples shimmer like silver chains. Dressed in light silk garments and with small fans in our hands, we sat side by side before the window overlooking the water. Above us, we saw clouds flying across the sky, transforming into myriad shapes.

"All the vastness of the universe shares this one same moon," Yun said, "I wonder if there are others in the world who are in a similar mood to ours tonight."

"Naturally there are people everywhere who also like to enjoy the moon on a breezy evening like this. There must also be many women inside embroidered doors of secluded boudoirs who are perceptive enough to appreciate the changing clouds in private," I replied, "As for a husband and wife viewing the moon together, I think their sentiments probably go beyond admiring these clouds."

---

26. Qixi, the seventh day of the seventh lunisolar month, often known today as the traditional Chinese equivalent of Valentine's Day.

Before long, the candles flickered out, while the moon sank lower in the sky. We cleared the fruits away and retired to bed.

On the full moon of the seventh month, commonly known as the Ghost Festival, Yun prepared some dishes, as we had planned to invite the moon to join us for a few drinks, but when night fell, the sky was suddenly overcast with dark clouds.

Looking troubled, Yun said, "If I am to grow old together with you, the moon must come out again."

I, too, felt disheartened. We could only see the distant fireflies on the opposite shore flicker like thousands of stars, threading their way through the willow-lined banks and smartweed-covered islets.

Yun and I began linking verses together to ease our gloom, but after just two rhymes, our couplets grew increasingly loose, our thoughts increasingly whimsical. Soon we found ourselves speaking nonsensically. Overcome by intense laughter and in tears, Yun collapsed into my arms, unable to utter a word. The intense fragrance of jasmine on her hair filled my nostrils. I gently patted her back and changed the topic:

"I had thought that women in ancient times adorned their hair with jasmine flowers because they resembled pearls. It did not occur to me that it is really because their fragrance is much lovelier when mixed with women's oils and powders, so much so that even the Buddha's hand should retreat three steps in comparison."

Yun stopped laughing and said, "The Buddha's hand is the gentleman of fragrances, its effect so subtle that it is only faintly discernible. Jasmine is the petty sort of fragrances and bolsters itself by borrowing from the advantages of another. Its fragrance is like the flattering smile of a sycophant."

"And how come you keep away from the gentleman and associate with the petty sort?" I said.

"Oh, I was only teasing a certain gentleman who favors a petty sort!" replied Yun.

Just as we were speaking, the water clock struck midnight. We watched as the wind gradually swept the clouds away, allowing the round, rolling moon to emerge. Overjoyed, we began drinking together by the window.

Barely three cups later, we suddenly heard a bang from below the bridge, as if someone had fallen into the river. We peered out the window, but the water's surface was smooth as a mirror, with nothing else in sight. Except we did hear the hurried sound of ducks scampering along the riverbank. I had long heard of a drowned ghost by the Pavilion, but did not say a thing lest Yun be frightened.

"Alas! Whence comes this noise?" exclaimed Yun.

We could not help but shudder. Hurriedly we closed the window and took the wine into our room. The flame in the lone lamp was small as a pea, and the curtains hung low. We were so fearful in that moment, an innocuous shadow might affright us. I trimmed the lamp's wick and placed it in the center of the room. Yun, however, had already come down with a high fever. I soon followed with the same, and we were both weak and fatigued for the next twenty days.

Truly it was as the saying goes, "Extreme joy brings disaster." This was also an omen that we would not grow old together.

It was soon the Mid-Autumn Festival, I had just recovered from my illness. Yun had been my wife for half a year now but still had never visited the Pavilion of Azure Waves next door. I thus instructed an old servant to arrange with the guard prior that no other visitors be let in. Toward evening, I set out with Yun and my younger sister, accompanied by a pair of maids old and young and with the old servant leading in front.

We crossed a stone bridge, turned east inside the gate, and followed a winding path tucked between large rocks and verdant trees. The pavilion itself stood atop a small hill. We climbed the steps to reach the pavilion's center, where one's view stretched several *li*.[27] All around, distant chimney smoke rose up from the cottages against the brilliant evening glow. On the opposite bank, there was a so-called "Forest by the Hill," and this was where high officials would entertain guests. By then Zhengyi Academy had yet to be established there.

We spread out a blanket we had brought in the pavilion and sat in a circle on the ground, whereas the guard brewed us some tea. Before long, the full moon had risen above the treetops, and we felt a gentle breeze beginning to rise beneath our sleeves. As the moon moved itself to the center of the water, all worldly concerns seemed to an instant.

"How enjoyable today's outing has been!" Yun exclaimed, "Wouldn't it be nice if we could take a small boat and drift beneath the Pavilion, too?"

By then the evening lamps had come on. Recalling our frightful experience on the fifteenth eve of the seventh month, we helped each other descend the pavilion and hurried home. In the local customs of Wu, women were free to go out on this night, regardless of the status of their families, and many would form groups to take strolls, a practice called "moonlight walk." Though the Pavilion was serene and elegant that night, no one else had come around here.

My father, Sir Jiafu, was fond of adopting sons.[28] Hence I have twenty-six brothers of different surnames. My mother also adopted nine daughters, among whom Missie Wang, the second, and Missie Yu, the sixth, got along best with Yun.

Wang was a giddy woman with a penchant for drinking, whereas Yu was gregarious and a great conversationalist. Whenever they got

---

27. One *li* is approximately a third of a mile.
28. Such adoptive relationships are akin to a secular version of the godparent-godson relationship.

together, they would always chase me out so that the three of them could sleep in the same bed. That was Missie Yu's idea alone. I once said with a laugh, "After sister you marry, I shall invite your husband to come stay for at least ten days straight." To which Yu replied, "Then I shall also come and sleep here with sister-in-law Yun. Wouldn't that be wonderful?" At this Yun and Wang only smiled.

After my brother Qitang also married, Yun and I moved to Granary Alley by the Bridge of Drinking Horse. The house there was more spacious in comparison, only that it lacked the graceful serenity of the Pavilion.

On my mother's birthday, a theater troupe came to perform. Yun watched in amazement at first. But my father did not have much sense of any inhibition and requested such tragic plays as *The Woeful Farewell*. The troupers portrayed the characters superbly, and all the viewers were moved. From behind the curtains I saw Yun get up abruptly and leave, not returning for a long time. I went in to find her, with Yu and Wang also following suit. We saw that Yun sat alone by the mirrored window with her chin propped in her hand.

"What has upset you so?" I asked.

"I had thought theater was for one's amusement," she answered. "But today's play only broke hearts!"

At her answer Yu and Wang both laughed. I said, "Here you have someone with great depths of feelings."

"Will sister-in-law sit alone here all day?" Yu asked.

"I will wait here for a play that is easier to endure," Yun answered.

Hearing this, Missie Wang first went out to ask my mother to request such plays like *Ciliang* and *Housuo*, and returned to urge Yun to go out to watch. Only then did Yun start to cheer.

Sir Sucun, my first cousin once removed, died young and had no children. My father hence named me his heir. His tomb is next to the ancestral graves on the Mountain of Blessing and Longevity in

West Kuatang. Every spring without fail, I would take Yun to sweep his tomb and pay homage. Missie Wang had heard that there was a Ge Garden nearby with beautiful views and for that reason asked to join us.

While there, Yun saw that the scattered stones on the ground had emerald patterns on them, mottled and pleasing to look at. She pointed them out to me, and said, "As tray rocks,[29] these stones might give more of a quaint and unique look than the white stones of Xuanzhou."

"Only I'm afraid these ones are hard to come by," I said.

At this Missie Wang offered, "If sister-in-law likes them so much, I can go gather her some."

She then borrowed from the gravekeeper a burlap sack and, with a lithe gait like that of a crane, started gathering stones. With each she picked up, if I answered, "Good," she would keep it; but if I said, "Nay," she would discard it.

Soon enough, sweat started dripping down her powdered face. She returned, lugging the sack behind her, and said, "If I gathered any more of these stones, I would collapse!"

Yun, while selecting the stones in the sack, said, "I heard that to harvest fruits in the mountains, one must get help from a monkey. It is really so."

At this an exasperated Missie Wang pinched her fingers together, making ready to tickle Yun. I put myself between them and reproached Yun, "You idled while she labored and yet you dared make such remarks. You can't blame sister for getting all ruffled."

On our way back, we toured Ge Garden, where tender green and delicate cerise vied for beauty. Wang, giddy as she always was, picked flowers whenever she came upon one.

---

29. Rocks used for *penshi,* the art form of creating miniature landscapes on trays using sand, pebbles, and small rocks (akin to the Japanese art of bonseki, which developed from *penshi*).

"You neither have a vase to put them in, nor do you wear them on your hair. What are you picking so many of them for?" Yun scolded her.

"Oh, what's the harm?" Wang replied. "It's not as if flowers know any pain!"

I laughed and said, "You will be damned to marry a pimpled, hairy man as redress for these flowers' grievances."

Giving me an angry look, Wang tossed the flowers onto the ground and kicked them into the pond with her tiny feet. "Why do you bully me like this?" she said. It took some good-humored mediation on Yun's part for her anger to subside.

Yun was at first quite reticent and preferred listening to me talk. I had to coax words out of her as one teases a cricket with a blade of grass, but gradually she began to speak more freely.

For her daily meals she always steeped her rice in tea, and she loved to eat fermented beancurd, or what we call "stinky beancurd" in Wu. She also loved cucumber pickled with prawn oil. These two things were the bane of my life, and I said in jest, "The dog, which has no stomach, eats excrement because it does not know stench, but the beetle, by way of rolling in dung, is transformed into a cicada because it aspires to fly high as it can. Which are you, a dog or a cicada?"

"I like fermented beancurd as it is inexpensive and goes well with rice and congee alike. Plus, I grew accustomed to eating it when I was a child," Yun replied. "Now that I have joined your household, like a dung beetle that has been transformed into a cicada, I still enjoy it because I'm not one to forget my origins. As for the pickled cucumber, I only tasted it for the first time when I moved here."

"In other words, my household is a dog's den?" I said.

Embarrassed, Yun tried to smooth it over, "Well, every household has its excrement, and the difference merely lies in whether one eats it or not. You enjoy garlic, so I force myself to eat it as well. I dare not force the beancurd on you, but the pickled cucumber—if you hold your breath to have a little taste—once it goes down, you'll understand how delicious it is. It is like Wuyan,[30] whose unattractive appearance belies her virtue."

"Are you trying to turn me into a dog, too?" I laughed and said.

"I have been a dog for a long while now," Yun said. "Why don't you deign to try it?"

She then stuck a piece into my mouth with her chopsticks. I chewed on it while pinching my nose and seemed to enjoy its sapid taste and crunchy texture. I then opened up my nostrils and had a few more, and to my surprise discovered yet a different flavor.

I have liked pickled cucumber ever since. Yun would mix sesame oil and sugar into the fermented beancurd, and I came to find that delectable, too. Or she would mash pickled cucumber and mix it with the beancurd, calling it the double fresh sauce, which had a peculiar tang to it.

"I don't understand how it is that I came to like something I detested so much at first," I said.

"You forgive the ugliness of something you love," said Yun.

The wife of my brother Qitang is the granddaughter of Master Wang Xuzhou. Back when their wedding day was approaching, she was short on pearl hairpins. Yun took out the ones she had received as a wedding gift and presented them to my mother, while the old maidservant lamented on the side. Yun explained, "It is in *yin* that all women inhere, and pearls themselves embody the essence of *yin*. Worn as jewelry, pearls might overpower any *yang* that is left, so why should I prize them so much?"

---

30. Zhongli Chun, who, according to legends, was an ugly woman who remained unmarried at age forty but was made queen consort of the State of Qi during the Warring States period (475–221 BCE) after she gave King Xuan counsel on governance.

Conversely, she treasured tattered books and ripped paintings exceedingly: if the books had missing parts, she would always sort them by category and then bind them together. She named these "Volumes of Mended Fragments." And when she came upon torn scrolls of calligraphy or painting, she would always patch them up with old paper and ask me to fill in any gaps. She named these "Collection of Deserted Delights."

Between embroidery and house chores, she busied herself all day with such minutiae and never tired of them. For her, finding an attractive slip of paper in some wretched trunk full of musty scripts and scrolls was like discovering a rare gem. Our old neighbor Lady Feng used to rack up such old scraps and sell them to her.

Yun had the same predilections as myself. She understood the intentions behind my eyes and the language of my brows, and she could thoroughly interpret any move or gesture, any subtle cue.

I once said to her, "It's a pity you are a woman and have to shelter at home. If only you could transform into a man, then we would be able to visit eminent mountains, seek out majestic ruins, and roam the whole country together. Wouldn't that be wonderful?"

"What's so difficult about that?" she replied. "Wait until my temples are gray. We might not be able to go as far as the Five Great Mountains, but Tiger Hill and the Mountain of Mystic Rock close by, the West Lake to the south of us, and Level Mountain to the north—these are all places we can visit together."

"I am afraid by the time your temples are gray, our footsteps will have gone weary," I said.

"If not in this lifetime, I hope we get to do so in the next," she said.

"In the next lifetime you should be a man," I said. "I will be a woman and follow you."

"And to make it even more romantic, we must not forget this lifetime," Yun added.

I laughed and said, "We still haven't finished talking about that congee we had when we were children. Should we not forget this lifetime in the next incarnation, we would not be able to shut our eyes on our wedding day, recounting all the events from the previous life."

"Legend has it that the Old Matchmaker of the Moon administers the matrimonial affairs of this world," Yun said. "He was kind enough to thread our fate together in this life, and our marriage in the next also depends on his divine powers. Why don't we make a painting of him and worship thereof?"

There was a Qi Liudi, courtesy name Zun, from Diaoxi, Zhejiang, who was adept at portraiture. We hence commissioned from him a painting. In it, the Matchmaker had his red thread in one hand, and in the other, a cane from which the Book of Marriages hangs. He had the face of a child and the hair of an old man, striding through what was neither smoke nor fog. Mr. Qi considered it one of his finest works.

Our friend Shi Zhuotang inscribed some words of paean at the top of the painting, which we hung in our inner chamber. On the first and fifteenth of every month, we husband and wife would always burn incense and pray thereunder. But later amidst vicissitudes in the family, the painting was somehow lost, and in whose home it lies now I do not know.

"Terminated is the present life, indeterminate the next." Are we two besotted lovers really going to be blessed by the divinities above?

When we moved to Granary Alley, I named our bedchamber "Court of Fragrant Guests," in reference to Yun's name[31] as well as the mutual courtesy we maintained, as if the other was a guest. The courtyard was narrow with high walls, with no view to speak of. A corridor in the back led to the library, where a window looked out to the abandoned Lu' family garden, quite a desolate sight.

---

31. Yun literally means the herb of grace, a fragrant plant.

The scenery at the Pavilion of Azure Waves still lingered on Yun's mind. East of Mother Gold's Bridge, to the north of Ridge Alley, there lived an old lady, whose cottage was surrounded by vegetable plots, with a woven fence as its gate. Beyond the gate, there was a pond about one *mu*[32] in size, with flowers and trees casting scattered shadows around the fence. This land used to be the site of the royal palace of Zhang Shicheng at the end of the Yuan dynasty.

Not too far to the west of the house, there was a mound made of rubble, from where one could gaze far into the distance. The surrounding area was sparsely populated, with a kind of unadorned beauty. The old lady had once mentioned her place in conversation, and Yun was very much captivated. She later told me, "Since leaving the Pavilion, I have often dreamed about going back, and have been considering what the next best thing might be, seeing we could not return. Why don't we go stay at the old lady's house?"

"The autumn heat has been scorching for several mornings in a row," I replied. "I've also been thinking of finding a cool place to while away the long days. If you wish, I'll first see if her home is suitable for staying, and then we can pack up our belongings and move there for a month. How does that sound?"

"But I'm afraid our parents will not permit this," said Yun.

I reassured her, "I'll ask them."

The next day, I went to the old lady's place. The cottage only had two proper rooms, made into four by a divider, but the paper windows and bamboo bed lent the dwelling a tranquil charm. The old lady understood my intention and gladly rented the bedchamber to us. Once the walls were pasted up with white paper, the room instantly looked refreshed. I then informed my mother and brought Yun to move in there.

---

32. One *mu* is approximately one sixth of an acre.

Our neighbors were only the old lady and her husband, who made a living from their gardens. They knew that we had come to escape the summer heat and greeted us with overflowing hospitality, offering us fish from the pond and vegetables from their garden. We tried to pay them, but they would not take it, so Yun made some shoes as gifts, and only then did the old couple accept our gesture of gratitude.

It was the midst of July, with lush trees casting dense shades, breezes gliding over the water, and cicadas loud in our ears. The old lady's husband also made a fishing rod for us, and we would often fish together in the recesses of the willow shade. At dusk we would climb up the mound to watch the sunset and evening clouds, composing linked verses when we felt so inclined, including such lines as:

Beast-cloud devours the setting sun;
Bow-moon launches the shooting star.

A while later, with the moon imprinting its image in the pond and the sounds of insects arising everywhere, we would set up a bamboo couch by the fence. The old lady would bring us warm wine and hot meals, and we would drink together in the moonlight and dine in a state of tipsiness.

After bathing, we would either sit or lie down in our sandals and with our banana leaf fans, listening to the old lady's husband tell tales of karma. By the third watch of the night,[33] we would retire to bed with our bodies thoroughly cooled, almost forgetting that we were in the city.

All around the fence there were chrysanthemums that the old lady had bought and replanted. The flowers would not bloom until the ninth month, so we ended up staying there for another ten days. My mother also gladly came to visit and brought some crabs for us

---

33. Between 11 p.m. and 1 a.m.

to enjoy as we spent the whole day admiring the chrysanthemums. Yun was delighted.

"In the future, the two of us should settle here," she said. "We can buy up ten *mu* of garden plots around the house and hire the old lady to help us grow vegetables and melons. You can paint, and I embroider, to provide expenses for the wine. Even with simple clothing and meals, we can live happily here for the rest of our life, with no need to make plans for distant travels."

I wholeheartedly agreed with her. But now, even if I were in possession of such a dwelling place, my intimate companion is long gone. Even the deepest sighs cannot convey the heaviness of my heart.

樂

Just a half *li* from my home, in the Vinegar Yard Alley, was the Shrine of Dongting,[34] commonly known as Narcissus Temple.

The temple had winding cloisters, as well as a few courtyards and pavilions. Upon a deity's birthday, the clans in the city would quietly claim a corner to hang a glass lantern, under which a throne and various flower vases would be laid out. The clans saw the quality of the floral arrangements and overall display as a matter of contest.

The daytime was reserved for various theatrical performances only, and it was in the evening that one could really tell better displays from the inferior ones: candles high and low would be placed among the vases in a practice called "floral illuminations," with smoke from the incense curling between the brightness of the flowers and the shadows of the lantern, creating the likeness of a night feast at the Dragon Palace.[35] Some of the temple's caretakers would be singing to the sound of *sheng* and *xiao*,[36] some chattering idly over tea they had

---

34. A shrine dedicated to water deities.
35. Where the Dragon King, a Chinese water and weather deity, resides.
36. Wind instruments.

brewed. Visitors thronged the temple like ants, so dense that barriers had to be set up under the eaves to prevent crowding.

By way of an invitation from a group of friends for me to help make floral arrangements, I got the opportunity to go witness the grand occasion. I told Yun about it at home, and she said, "It's a pity I'm not a man and cannot go with you."

"We can dress you in my gown and crown you with my cap," I replied. "Whence a woman is into a man transformed."

Accordingly, we changed her coiffure into a queue[37] and brushed makeup on her brows to make them thicker. With my cap on, only a little hair at her temples was showing, passing off just well enough. But my gown was one and a half *cun*[38] too long. We thus folded the gown at the waist, sewed it up, and put on a jacket over it.

"And what are we going to do about my feet?" Yun asked.

"There are these butterfly shoes in the marketplace, adjustable in size and readily purchasable," I answered. "You can wear them as slippers as well in the morning and evening. Wouldn't that be good?"

Yun gladly agreed. After dinner, when she was fully dressed, she paced about for quite some time, imitating the gestures and stride of a man. But then she had a sudden change of heart.

"I won't go after all," she declared. "If someone recognizes me and your parents get word of this, it will be trouble."

"Who doesn't know me at the temple? If they recognize us, they will just laugh it off," I said, as encouragement. "My mother is in the home of my ninth sister's husband at present. Also, the place will be thronged with visitors, how should anyone know we are there?"

Yun then fetched a mirror. Looking at her reflection, she started laughing uncontrollably. I pulled her toward me and we sneaked out together.

---

37. Male hairstyle worn in Qing China, featuring a shaved front scalp and braid in the back.
38. One *cun* is approximately one and a quarter inches.

We roamed the temple freely and no one noticed that she was a woman. When asked who she was, I would say she was my cousin, with her only responding with a polite clasp of the hands.

Toward the end, we came to a place where a young woman and her little girl were seated behind the ceremonial display. These were the kin of one of the temple's caretakers surnamed Yang. Yun approached them quite abruptly to greet them, but as she turned, she placed her hand on the young woman's shoulder by accident. A maidservant on the side got up angrily and shouted, "Who's this bold fellow, acting with such impropriety?"

Just as I was trying to come up with an excuse to smooth things over, Yun, seeing the situation desperate, promptly removed her cap and revealed her feet, saying, "I am a woman, too!" Astounded, the women's anger passed into amusement. They invited us to stay for tea and snacks, and arranged for a sedan chair to carry us home.

When Qian Shizhu of Wujiang died of illness, my father wrote home, instructing me to go offer my condolences. Yun said to me in private, "One must pass through Taihu Lake[39] on their way to Wujiang. I wish to accompany you on this trip so I can expand my horizons."

I replied, "I was just getting worried about feeling lonely during my travels. Having you join me would certainly be nice, but I can't think of an excuse."

"I can say I'm paying a visit to my maiden home," she said. "You go ahead and board the boat first, and I will follow shortly after."

"If so, on the way back, we can make fast our boat beneath the Bridge of Myriad Years and enjoy a cool evening there under the moon, as a postlude to our romantic affairs at the Azure Waves," I offered.

---

39. Literally, Lake Immense. The third greatest lake in China.

It was the eighteenth of June, a cool morning. I set off first with a servant to the ferry at River Xu, where we boarded the boat and waited for Yun. Sure enough, she arrived anon in a sedan chair. We unfastened the boat and passed through the Bridge of Tiger's Roar, whereupon wind-sails and sand-birds came gradually into view. The water and sky merged into one unified color.

"Ah! Is this why they call it Lake Immense?" Yun exclaimed. "Now that I've seen the vastness of heaven and earth, I can say I have not lived my life in vain. But imagine how few ladies in their lifetime are able to witness such a sight!"

We engaged in some more idle chatter and soon saw the wind stirring willows on the bank. We had arrived at the city of Wujiang.

After attending the memorial ashore, I returned to find the boat empty. Worried, I inquired with the boatman, who pointed and said, "Do you not see the person on the long bridge in the willow shade, watching the cormorants hunt fish?"

It turned out that Yun had disembarked with the boatman's daughter. When I approached them from behind, I saw that she was perspiring all over her powdered face, gazing into the distance as she leaned on the girl. I tapped her on the shoulder and said, "Your gown is soaked through with sweat!"

Yun turned around and replied, "I was afraid someone from the Qian family might come to the boat, so I thought I'd hide away for a while. How come you returned so quickly?"

I laughed and answered, "To catch the fugitive."

We then took each other's arm and boarded the boat again, rowing back toward the Bridge of Myriad Years. The sun was still up, and all the boat's windows were let down to allow the gentle breeze in. Yun was dressed in a soft, silky gown, swaying a feathered fan in her hand. The boatman sliced up a watermelon to help cool us down.

The sun set only moments later, casting a red hue upon the side of the bridge, and the evening haze shrouded the riverside willows in twilight. The moon was yet to rise, but the river was already brimming with lights from the fishing boats.

I told the servant to go astern and have a drink with the boatman. As for the boatman's daughter, her name was Suyun, and we had had a drink together once—she was a pleasant girl. I beckoned her to come sit with Yun. We did not light up the lantern by the bow, but instead waited for the moon to rise and played "shooting the hidden" with wine as wagers. The wine cups were constantly being refilled.

A bright-eyed Suyun, after observing our game for some while, said, "I am quite familiar with drinking games but had never heard of this one. I'd like to learn."

Yun thus started explaining the game with some analogies, but Suyun was still confused. I laughed and said, "Will the lady teacher pause for a moment? I have an analogy that should make clear the rules at once."

"How would you explain then!"

"The crane dances but cannot plow. The buffalo plows but cannot dance. Every animal is bound by its nature," I said. "If a teacher goes against someone's nature in her instruction, isn't that merely useless effort?"

Suyun laughed and, striking me playfully on the shoulder, said, "Are you calling me a buffalo?"

"Words only, no hands!" Yun ordered. "Whoever violates this rule drinks a big cup of wine."

Suyun was a great drinker, so she filled up a big cup and guzzled it down in one gulp.

"Hands are fine, but only for caressing, not for striking," I said.

Laughing Yun pulled Suyun into my arms and said, "Alright then, you can caress away."

"You don't understand," I said, also laughing. "The essence of a caress lies in its subtlety, in its being between intention and accident. A full embrace and frenzied groping is the way of a country bumpkin."

At this moment their jasmine hairpins, mixed with the scent of wine and sweat-melted makeup, exuded a strong aroma. I joked, "The stench of a petty sort is overwhelming this side of the boat, making me feel ill."

At this, Suyun clenched up her fists and struck me several more times, "Who told you to sniff around like that?"

"Two cups for violating the rule!" Yun cried out.

"He called me a petty sort. Why shouldn't I strike him?" Suyun objected.

"The petty sort he was referring to means something else," Yun said. "Pray drink these, and I will tell you."

After Suyun guzzled up the two cups, Yun told her the story from that cool evening when we still resided at the Azure Waves.

"If that is the case, I was indeed in the wrong. I shall take another penalty!" Suyun said as she drank up another cup.

Yun continued, "I had long heard that Lady Su was a great singer. May we have the pleasure of hearing your beautiful voice?"

Su complied, singing to the percussion of her ivory chopsticks on the dishes. A delighted Yun drank to her heart's content and was intoxicated before long, so I sent her home first in a sedan chair. I stayed to chat with Suyun some more over tea and afterward walked home under the moon.

At the time, we were staying with our friend Lu Banfang at his Free and Easy House. Several days later, Madam Lu, having caught a rumor, told Yun in private, "The other day I heard that your husband took two courtesans to drink in a boat by the Bridge of Myriad Years. Did you know this?"

"Yes, that did happen," Yun replied. "And one of those two was me."

She then told Madam Lu the whole story about our travels.

Madam Lu laughed and left at ease.

In the seventh month of Jia Yin during Emperor Qianlong's reign,[40] I returned home from the eastern part of Guangdong. One of my companions, my cousin-in-law Xu Xiufeng, brought home a concubine. He boasted about her beauty profusely and invited Yun to admire her. Later, Yun told Xu Xiufeng, "She is indeed beautiful, but still lacks grace."

"Then if a gentleman were to take a concubine, must she be both beautiful and graceful?" Xiufeng asked.

"Yes," Yun replied.

From that point on, she became obsessed with searching for such a woman for me, but we were constrained in funds.

At that time, there was a courtesan from Zhejiang named Wen Lengxiang,[41] who was residing in Wu. She had composed four poems about willow catkins in regulated verse, which quickly gained fame in the region, leading many admirers to compose their own poems in reply.

My friend Zhang Xianhan[42] from Wujiang, who had long admired Lengxiang, came to me with the willow catkins poem in hopes that I would help compose a reply. Yun did not think much of Xianhan and so did not so much look at the poem, but I, itching to write, composed one in response. Yun was particularly impressed with this couplet:

These lithe flutters brush on my spring sorrow;
Drifting astray, they stir up her heart's longing.

The following autumn, on the fifth day of the eighth month in the year Yi Mao,[43] my mother was just about to take Yun out on an excursion to Tiger Hill when Xianhan suddenly turned up at our doorsteps.

---

40. 1794.
41. Lengxiang: Literally, cold fragrance.
42. Xianhan: Literally, idle and simple.
43. 1795.

"I, too, am on my way to Tiger Hill, and I specially invite you to act as an envoy today to explore some flowers," he said to me.

I asked my mother to go ahead and meet us at Half Pond by Tiger Hill. Meanwhile, my friend took me to Lengxiang's residence. I discovered she was already middle-aged and had a daughter named Hanyuan.

The daughter was not yet of marriageable age but already tall and graceful, giving an air of, precisely as described in that verse, "an expanse of autumn water chills one with its cold reflection." From talking to her, I gleaned that she was rather knowledgeable in the literary arts. She also had a little sister named Wenyuan.

I went in with no wishful delusion, knowing fully that an impoverished scholar like myself would not be able to afford even a fragment of her time. I secretly felt quite uneasy in the midst but still forced myself to partake in conversation.

I said to Xianhan in private, "I am but a poor scholar. Are you teasing me with these charming women?"

"Not at all," Xianhan laughed and replied. "A friend invited me to Hanyuan's place to return a favor, but our hostess insisted on me bringing a distinguished guest. I merely extended the invitation as a guest myself, so don't worry about anything else."

Only then did I feel relieved. When on Half Pond our two boats met, I asked Hanyuan to go to the other boat to meet my mother.

Yun and Han took an immediate fancy to each other, as if they had been old friends, and hand-in-hand they climbed the hill to see all the famous sights. Yun especially loved the vast vistas seen from the heights of Thousand-Acre Cloud and sat there for quite some time in admiration of the scenery.

On our return to the Shore of Rural Flores, we made merry with copious amounts of wine, having made fast our two boats side by side. Just as we were about to set forth again, Yun said to me, "How about you go with Mr. Zhang and leave Han with me?" I agreed.

It was not until we passed the Inner City Bridge that we returned to our own boat and parted ways. When we got home it was already the third watch of the night.

"I finally found someone with both beauty and grace today," Yun said. "I've already made plans for Hanyuan to visit tomorrow. I will arrange everything for you."

I was aghast.

"One cannot keep such a woman without a golden mansion," I said. "As an impoverished scholar, how dare I entertain such a fantasy? Moreover, our bond as husband and wife is deep and steadfast. Why should I look elsewhere?"

"Oh, but *I* love her!" Yun laughed and said. "Just leave the matter to me."

The following day at high noon, Hanyuan arrived sure enough. Yun was particularly hospitable, and we feasted and played the finger guessing game, with the winner reciting poems and the loser imbibing wine. Throughout dinner, Yun said not a word of solicitation.

After Hanyuan had gone home, Yun said, "I have discreetly made another appointment for her to come on the eighteenth, when we will become sworn sisters. You should prepare livestock and offerings to receive her."

She then smiled and pointed to the emerald bracelet on her arm, saying, "If you see this bracelet on Hanyuan, it means the matter will come to fruition. I have hinted at my intent, though I do not yet know where her heart lies." I only listened but made no reply.

There was a downpour on the eighteenth, but Hanyuan actually braced the rain to make the appointment. The two of them stayed in the inner chamber for a long time before re-emerging hand-in-hand before me. Han[44] looked somewhat embarrassed. It turned out that

---

44. Hanyuan.

the emerald jade had already found its way onto her arm.

After they burned incense together to pledge themselves as sisters, we intended to play the drinking game again like last time, but it just so happened that Hanyuan was going on a trip to Stone Lake and so had to depart.

A delighted Yun said to me, "Now that the beauty is secured, how are you going to thank the matchmaker?"

I asked her to elaborate, and she replied, "Just now I had to speak to her in private first as I feared her heart already belonged to someone else. But I soon discovered there was no other and so said to her, 'Sister, do you understand my intent today?'

"To which she replied, 'To be favored by an honorable lady like yourself truly makes me feel like a humble reed leaning up against a majestic tree. Only my mother expects me to live a life of luxury, and I fear that my own fate is not up to me. I hope we can deliberate and find a way.'

"And as I took off my emerald bracelet and put it on her, I counseled her, 'Jade is prized for its unwavering strength, and its circumference symbolizes unbroken union. Try wearing it first, sister, as a good omen.'

"To which she answered, 'The power to unite us rests with you, Madam.' Judging from this, you already have Hanyuan's heart, and any difficulty lies only with Lengxiang. We must plan further."

I laughed and asked her, "Are you trying to emulate Liweng's *The Fragrant Companions*?"[45]

"Exactly right," she replied.

Since then a day did not go by without her speaking of Hanyuan.

---

45. *The Fragrant Companions*: Play by Li Yu (1611–1680) literary name Liweng (literally, bamboo-hatted old man). Known as the most significant work of premodern Chinese literature that portrays a sapphic relationship, the play tells of a story of two women falling in love after meeting at a nunnery and exchanging poems with each other, who come together through a legitimate marriage—with the same husband.

But later Hanyuan was taken off by a powerful man, and all our plans came to naught. And of all things, this might have been the final cause of Yun's death.

RECORD OF IDLE PLEASURES

I recall that when I was a child, I could open my eyes wide toward the sun and make out the smallest of specks. Whenever I came upon a minuscule object, I would always examine its fine lines and patterns closely, from which I was able to derive pleasure outside of the thing itself.

Summer mosquitoes often swarmed like thunder, and privately I would equate them with flocks of cranes dancing in the sky. And where the heart intended, there were really cranes in the hundreds or thousands. I would look up at them until my neck stiffened.

Or I would keep some mosquitoes inside my white curtain[46] and slowly puff smoke onto them so that they would soar against it. I watched them as if they were white cranes amidst blue clouds, where sure enough like cranes they bugled. At this I would let out exclamations of delight.

And at some jagged spot of a clay wall by a flower-bed covered by weeds, I would often squat down so that I was level with the flower-bed itself and look closely. Weeds became forests, ants and bugs beasts; the little protrusions on the ground were hills and hollow valleys. My spirit wandered therein, contented.

One day, I saw two insects battling in the grass. Just as I was fully absorbed in the spectacle, some behemoth appeared out of nowhere, uprooting hills and tearing down trees along the way—it was a toad. One flick of the tongue and the two bugs were devoured. Being so young and engrossed in the scene as I was, I cried out loud in horror. After I had collected myself, I caught the toad, whipped it several dozen times, and chased it into another yard.

Reflecting back on it when I was older, what really happened in the two insects' fight was one attempting rape, the other resisting.

---

46. Mosquito net.

The ancient proverb goes, "Fornication draws death near." Is it the same for insects, too?

I was so easily transfixed by this sort of activity that my egg (in the Wu dialect we call those male parts "eggs") was once sucked on by an earthworm and became so swollen I could not urinate.[47] A duck was caught to suck on it with its mouth held open,[48] but the maid accidentally let go of her hand, and the duck jolted its neck as if about to swallow. I screamed in fright; a laughingstock since.

These were all things that pleased me as a child.

As I got older, I became an anthophile to the point of obsession, and loved pruning potted trees.[49] But it was not until I got to know Zhang Lanbo that I really started honing the craft of pruning branches and nurturing joints, and still later the art of graftage and rockery.

The orchid is the most prized of flowers because of its subdued fragrance and graceful charm. Yet varieties even mildly worthy of catalog are hard to come by.

At the end of his days, Lanbo gifted me a spring orchid with lotus-like petals and a white heart. Its shoulders[50] were even, its heart broad. The stems were slender, petals neat. It belonged in a catalog, and I treasured it like a piece of expensive jade.

When I was working away from home, Yun would water it herself, and its flowers and leaves grew luxuriantly. Yet in less than two years

---

47. During Shen Fu's time young boys wore crotchless bottoms. Here, the earthworm bite probably occurred while Shen's younger self was squatting down in the grass with his private parts exposed.
48. It was believed that the saliva of ducks could cure the ailment at issue.
49. Potted trees: *Penzai*, or *penjing*, the Chinese traditional practice of growing and shaping miniature trees planted in pots (akin to the Japanese art of bonsai, which developed from *penzai*).
50. The lateral sepals of an orchid.

it wilted and died all of a sudden. I dug up its roots to look, only to find that they were all white as jade, with new growths quite robust.

At first I could not understand this and, with long sighs, resigned to the thought that perhaps such a delicate plant was just beyond my fortune. Only later did I learn that someone who had asked for, but been refused, a cutting killed it by pouring boiling water over it. I swore that from then on I would never grow orchids again.

Next of my favorites was the azalea. Though it did not have much fragrance to speak of, its colors were enduring and pleasing to look at. It was also easy to prune. Except Yun loved each branch and pitied each leaf too much to trim them freely, so it was difficult to give them great form. The same thing was true for all my other potted trees.

Only chrysanthemums, which would bloom every year east of our fence, were the true object of our autumnal passion. I much preferred to pick them and place them in vases rather than raising them in pots—not that I did not like them in pots, but because our gardenless predicament did not permit us to grow them in that manner. The ones from the market, all unkempt like weeds, were not to our liking.

When arranging chrysanthemums, one should have the flowers in odd rather than even numbers. Each vase should have only one color. The mouth of the vase should be broad rather than narrow, so that the flowers can unfurl without constraint.

Whether there be five or seven flowers or a few dozen, the flowers should rise from the mouth of the vase in one straight bunch, neither too loose nor overcrowded, nor should they lean against the mouth of the vase. This is called "keeping the handle firm."

The flowers may stand gracefully straight, or else spread out at different angles. Some should be tall, some should be low, with a few buds mixed in, so as to avoid the uncomely look of a platter. The leaves should not be disorderly, and the stems should not be stiff. If needles are used to keep the stems in place, any extra lengths should be clipped off so that they are not visible. This is called "keeping the mouth clear."

Depending on the size of the table, three to seven vases should suffice. Any more, one would not be able to make out the contours of each bunch, making them no different than those tawdry chrysanthemum screens sold at the markets.

The stands for the vases can be anywhere between three or four inches to two feet and five or six inches tall. They should vary in height but call to each other, forming a concerted composition. If the stands in the center are uniformly tall and the ones on the sides are low, or if the ones in the back are all tall, the ones in the front all low, the arrangement would look too symmetrical, or what we commonly call "a heap of brilliant refuse." Whether they should be densely arranged or spread out, leaning toward or away from the viewer, is a question left to one's pictorial sensibility.

If instead basins, plates, or bowls are used, one can mix pitch, rosin, elm bark, flour, and oil together and heat the mixture along with rice stalk ash until it congeals into a glue. Press pins onto a copper plate with the pins facing upward, and melt the glue to stick the plate to the basin, plate, or bowl. After the glue has cooled, tie up a bunch of flowers with thin wire and affix them to the pins.

The bunch is better aslant, rather than shooting up straight from the center. Sparse branches and tidy leaves serve best. Clutter is to be avoided. Then add water, and use a little sand to conceal the copper plate, so that the flowers seem to the viewer to have grown directly from the bottom of the bowl.

If flowers or fruits from woody plants are used for arrangement, one must first trim them (for one cannot pick every kind of flower oneself, and those picked by others tend to be unsatisfactory). With a branch in hand, tilt it up and down, turn it back and forth, and see how it looks best. After that's decided, cut off the superfluous twigs for a look that is slim, spare and strange.

Next consider how the stem should enter the vase, with what kind of bend and curve, so that when one puts the branches in, one can avoid the pitfall of having the leaves backwards and the blossoms sideways. If one simply takes any branch that comes to hand and places it upright into a vase, the main stem will look stiff, the branches disorderly, with blossoms sideways and leaves backwards, such that the whole will look devoid of any grace and refinement.

And here's how to curve an otherwise straight stem: make a cut in the middle of it and insert a small piece of rock therein; what was straight now has an inflection. One can also beat a couple of pins to fix it in place lest the stem fall over. Maple leaves and bamboo twigs, or even weeds and brambles, can all be arranged in this manner.

Or, take a green stem of bamboo and pair it with some goji berries, a few blades of thin grass, as well as a couple vines of brambles, and one may derive from it some unearthly delight, as long as the arrangement is appropriate.

趣

When planting new trees and flowers, one might as well plant them askew so as to take advantage of gravity. Let the plants face where they will, and after a year their branches will grow upright again. If all the trees are planted straight up, one will not be able to make use of gravity that way.

As for pruning potted trees, first take those with claw-like roots exposed, cut off excess branches so as to group the rest into three sections from left to right, and let the top grow. Each time the main stem branches off, leave only one branch. Allow seven such branches, or nine, unto the top. It is in poor taste to have canopies directly opposite each other like a pair of shoulders and arms, or to have the joints of the stem swollen like a crane's knees.

The branches must go out in a spiral, rather than simply alternate left and right, which would give the tree an unattractive look, as if it had a bare chest and exposed back. Nor should the branches grow only from the front and the back. There are also potted trees, so-called "double trunked" or "treble trunked," with two or three upward growths from the same roots. But if the roots of a tree were not claw-shaped, it would look like it was crudely stuck into the dirt and would on that ground be disqualified.

The proper training of a tree, however, takes at least thirty to forty years. In my lifetime I have only seen one man who has succeeded in training several such trees, old Wan Caizhang of my home county. I have also seen, at a merchant's in Yangzhou, one boxwood and one cedar, both gifted by a visitor from Yushan, like pearls before swine—ill-considered, I would say.

Another thing: a tree with its trunk and canopies shaped like a pagoda, or branches curled like earthworms, would look far too trite.

Ornament the pot with flowers and stones to make small picturesque scenes, or grand scenes of enchantment. If, with a cup of green tea, one could easily transport oneself into the scene, that is a sign of an arrangement fit for fine enjoyment in one's private studio.

Once, I planted some narcissus but had no stones from Lingbi to pair them with, so I tried substituting them with pieces of charcoal that looked like stones. One could also take five or seven differently-sized cabbage hearts, of a color white as jade, and plant them in sand in a rectangular pot, again using pieces of charcoal in place of stones to decorate. This arrangement would lend an effect chiaroscuro quite interesting to look at.

Thinking along these lines provides one with infinite possibilities of pleasure, and it's difficult to enumerate them all. For instance, if one chews some calamus seeds along with cold rice broth, and blows the mixture onto bits of charcoal which are then put in a dark and damp place, fine little calamus will grow therein. These can then be easily moved to a pot or a bowl, fluffy and lovely to look at.

Or, thin both ends of some old lotus seeds and put them into an eggshell, place it under a hen with her other eggs, and take it out when the chicks hatch. Plant the seeds in a small pot using clay from an old swallow's nest, adding in two-tenths of asparagus, and ground well. Water the seeds with river water and light them with morning sun. When the flowers bloom they will be only as big as a wine cup, and the leaves will have shrunk to the size of a bowl, elegant and lovely to look at.

趣

When it comes to the layout of garden pavilions, nested rooms, winding corridors, and the correspondent landscape design with rockery and flowers and greenery, one should try to evoke the small in the large, and the large in the small; to have the real in the illusion, the illusory in the real; to conceal as well as reveal, with recesses now shallow, now deep. Arranging a proper garden is not as simple a matter as creating patterns of tortuosity, nor is the larger, or the fuller, the better—operating under such a misconception would only result in wasted time and energy.

A miniature mountain can be made from a pile of dirt dug out from the ground, to be ornamented with stones and bedecked with plants. One could use plum branches as benches, vines as walls. This way, a mountain is made where once there was naught.

To evoke the small in the large, one could, for instance, populate an open area with easy-growing bamboos, only to screen them off with lush plum trees in front. To evoke the large in the small, make the wall of a narrow garden jagged; green it with vines growing from the corner of the wall and embed it with large rocks, complete with inscriptions. Then, upon opening the window, one would feel as if he was looking out to a cliff, across endless precipices.

To have the real in the illusion means, for instance, at the end of a winding path, where mountains are exhausted and waters reach an end, having a sudden turn reveal an expansive vista; or, similarly, by a dining area situated within a pavilion, having a door open to another courtyard. To have the illusory in the real means, for example, to have only a closed courtyard behind another door, arrayed in bamboo and rockery, creating the semblance of a passage where there is none; or, similarly, having a low railing set up atop a wall to give the illusion of a platform above.

A poor scholar's dwelling often has fewer rooms than is demanded. One might want to draw from the layout seen in the stern of a Taiping boat of my home county, with modifications. In such a layout, cascading steps, with the additional space in the front and back, can be made into three beds, separated by paper-covered boards. Such a construction, layered yet well-partitioned, gives the feeling of a walk down a long road, its narrowness easily overlooked.

When we lived in Yangzhou, Yun and I employed this exact method. Though the house only spanned two beams,[51] our two sleeping quarters, kitchen, and living area were all independent of each other, with space to spare. Yun once remarked laughingly: "This layout is exquisite enough, but the grandeur of a wealthy household it has not!" It was certainly so.

Once, while sweeping our ancestral graves in the mountains, I discovered some stones with patterns like undulating hills. When I returned home, I discussed these finds with Yun:

"We use white putty to set Xuanzhou stones in our stone basins because the colors are uniform. The yellow stones from this mountain are quaint and lovely. But if we also use putty to affix them, the contrast between the yellow and the white will make the work all too visible. What shall we do?"

---

51. Meaning the house only had two beams. While this is not a strict form of measurement, the number of beams is often referred to in order to indicate the size of a dwelling.

"Pick some inferior stones," Yun replied, "grind them into powder and paste a wet mixture of it onto where the putty is. When it dries, perhaps the colors will blend nicely together."

I did as she suggested, using a rectangular basin from the Yixing kiln to raise a peak, slanted to the left and protruding from the right, with horizontal patterns on the back resembling those from the paintings of Yunlin.[52] The rocks were rugged like cliffs over a river. We filled an empty corner with river mud and planted therein frogbit with many white petals; onto the stones, we grew cypress vines, commonly known as cloud pine. This took quite a few days to complete.

By late fall, the cypress vines had crept over the entire peak, resembling wisteria hanging from a cliff. Their blossoms were a true red. Meanwhile, the white flowers of the frogbit had also breached the surface of the water in full bloom. Letting our spirits wander therein, we felt as if we had ascended the immortal islands of Penglai.

Placing this arrangement under our eaves, Yun and I observed: here we could add a pavilion on the water, and here a thatched gazebo; this spot calls for a six-word inscription that reads, *Between Falling Flowers and Flowing Water*; we could dwell here, fish here, and gaze into the distance here. Our hearts were full with such visions, as if we were really moving into those mountains.

One evening, the cats were fighting over food and fell from the eaves. The whole thing, basin and all, was shattered in a mere instant. I sighed and said, "To think a design as small as ours could offend the Creator!" The two of us could not help but shed tears.

In burning incense in a quiet room lies another cultivated pleasure of the leisurely life. Yun used to steam agarwood, aquilaria, and other fragrant woods in a rice cauldron, and then place them on a brass wire rack above the stove, about an inch from the heart of the fire. The

---

52. Ni Zan (1301–1374), painter of the Yuan and Ming dynasties, known for the sparse style of his landscape paintings.

scent produced by the slow burn had a subtle charm and was free of any smoke.

The Buddha's hand should not be smelled by a drunken man, or it will spoil easily. It is also bad for the quince to perspire, and if it does, it must be washed with water. Only the *shangjuan*[53] has no such care requirements. The Buddha's hand and the quince both call for special preservation, but I shall go into detail here. Let's just say that whenever we saw someone thoughtlessly take up one of these things to smell them and then just as thoughtlessly putting it down, we would know they did not understand the art of preserving them.

When living at home, the vase on my desk is never empty of flowers. Yun once said to me, "You have made flower arrangements that go with all elements of weather—wind, sun, rain, and dew; they are truly exquisite. Now there is also a school of painting that specializes in insects and grasses—why don't you try emulating that?"

"Insects are too restless to be contained," I replied. "So how should I emulate those paintings?"

"There is a method, but I fear it would set a cruel precedent," Yun responded.

"Try telling me."

She went, "The color of an insect does not change even as it dies. One can find a praying mantis, cicada, butterfly, or the like, kill it with a needle, and use fine thread to tie its neck to the flowers and grasses, arranging its legs to either cling to a stem or rest on a leaf, as though it was still alive. Wouldn't that work?"

I was delighted and did as she suggested. Everyone who saw it had to praise it. I suspect a woman with such perceptive sensibilities is hard to come by these days.

---

53. Cold-hardy citrus fruit.

Yun and I also stayed with the Huas in Xishan for a while, during which time Madam Hua had Yun teach her two daughters to read. The courtyard of that country house was spacious and empty. In the summer the sun would feel oppressive, and so Yun taught the family how to make movable flower screens that were quite ingenious.

Each screen had a base that was made from two wooden branches about four or five inches long, fashioned like low benches, with an open space in the center, divided by four horizontal bars approximately a foot apart. Round openings were drilled in the four corners for the installation of bamboo lattices. The screens stood about six or seven feet tall. She then planted some hyacinth beans in sand pots and placed them inside the screens, allowing the vines to climb up the lattices. Two people could easily move the screens.

One can make several more of these screens and place them wherever he pleases, creating the effect of a window shaded by green: sun out, breezes in. The screens can be arranged in a meandering manner, and the plants can be changed at any time, hence the name movable flower screens. With this method, any flowering vines seen in the area can be made use of, a great way to rejoice in the rural way of life.

趣

I had a friend, Lu Banfang, whose given name was Zhang, courtesy name Chunshan. He was a skilled painter of pines and cypresses, and of plums and chrysanthemums. He was also well-versed in cursive script as well as seal carving. I lived in his home, Free and Easy House, for a year and a half.

The house faced east and spanned five beams, with our living quarters occupying the three in the back. Whether it was bright or gloomy, windy, or rainy, we always had a great view looking out to the distant landscapes. In the courtyard, there was an osmanthus tree, which exuded an enchanting fragrance, and the house had corridors connecting its different wings, all very secluded and quiet.

When we moved in, a servant and a maid, along with their little girl, came as well. The man could make clothes, and the maid could spin. So Yun would embroider, the maid spun, and the man made garments to provide for ourselves.

I have always enjoyed entertaining guests, and whenever we drank together, we would always play drinking games. Yun was adept at cooking up a feast within the constraints of our means. Squash, vegetables, fish, or shrimp, once touched by her, would all take on delightfully surprising flavors. My friends, knowing I was poor, would often contribute some wine money so we could talk the whole day away.

I have always been keen on cleanliness. My space was free of dust and lint but had a relaxed atmosphere, allowing guests to carry themselves freely. Among my visitors was Yang Bufan, given name Changxu, known for his portraits; Yuan Shaoyu, given name Pei, skilled in landscape painting; and Wang Xinglan, given name Yan, adept in landscape painting; Wang Xinglan, given name Yan, whose specialty was flowers and feathers.

All of them loved Free and Easy House for its elegance and would come with their painting supplies. I learned to paint from them, as well as calligraphy, seal carving, from which we made some extra cash that was turned over to Yun, who bought tea and wine for our guests. All day we would talk about poetry and art and nothing more.

There were also the Xia Dan'an and Yi Shan brothers, the Miao Shanyin and Zhi Bai brothers, along with other scholars like Jiang Yunxiang, Lu Juxiang, Zhou Xiaoxia, Guo Xiaoyu, Hua Xingfan, and Zhang Xianhan. All of them came and went like swallows on a beam.

Yun would even sell her hairpins for wine without a second thought, because we could not bear to squander such fine moments and beautiful scenery. Yet now we are all scattered in different places, like clouds parted by the wind. The woman I loved is gone; jade broken, incense buried. How hard it is to look back! Is this not what they mean by "once a common sight, now a source of grief"?

Free and Easy House had four prohibitions: discussions of official promotions, bureaucratic affairs, or the eight-legged essay style,[54] and gambling on card games or dice. Anyone who violated these rules would pay a fine of five jugs of wine. On the other hand, there were four values we all endorsed: generosity and enthusiasm, romanticism in refinement, a carefree and unrestrained spirit, and tranquility and clarity.

During the long summer days with little to do, we would hold "examinations" among ourselves. Each examination would have eight participants, with each bringing two hundred copper coins.

First, we would draw lots: the one who drew the first lot would be the examiner, seated at the front, while the second would be the recorder, also seated in his assigned place. The others would then be the candidates, each taking a paper slip from the recorder, properly stamped with the recorder's seal. The examiner would give out, as prompts, five heptasyllabic couplets and five pentasyllabic couplets. The candidates were allotted the time it took to burn one incense stick to think and compose their couplets. No discussion was allowed.

Once completed, the candidates would submit their work into a box and take their seat. After all submissions were in, the recorder would open the box, copy the writings onto a booklet, and present them to the examiner, who would review them blind so as to prevent any personal bias.

From the sixteen pairs of couplets, three heptasyllabic ones and three pentasyllabic ones would be selected. The one with the best couplets would be appointed as the next host, while the second would serve as the recorder. Those who did not have any couplets selected

---

54. The style of essay used in imperial examinations during the Ming and Qing dynasties.

would pay twenty in cash; those who had one selected would pay ten, and anyone exceeding the time limit would pay double the fee. In a single session, the examiner could earn a hundred in "incense fees."

In a day, we could hold as many as ten sessions, collecting some one thousand in cash, a great gain for our wine fund. Only Yun received the "preferred paper" treatment — she had the privilege to think and compose on her own time.

One day, Yang Bufan did a sketch of me and Yun planting flowers in the garden, in vivid likeness. That evening, the moon showed a nice complexion, and the shadow of orchids climbed up our pink wall; quite the serene grace. Xinglan, intoxicated as well as inspired, said, "Bufan can sketch your portraits. And I can paint these flowers' shadows." I laughed and said, "But can you paint them as well as we were sketched?"

Xinglan then took a piece of plain paper and pasted it on to the wall, where he traced the orchids' shadows in ink now dark, now light. We took a proper look at it the next day, and while it was not so much a real painting, the sparse lines of flowers and leaves were indeed enchanting like that moonlit scene. Yun cherished it very much, and we each wrote an inscription on it.

In Suzhou, there are two gardens: the South Garden and the North Garden. As when the rapeseed flowers were in bloom, it became quite a problem that there was no tavern closeby for us to get a leisurely drink. If we brought our own picnic basket, only to toast the flowers with cold wine, that would be no fun at all.[55] Some suggested buying wine from the nearest tavern. Others proposed going for drinks after viewing the flowers. But neither seemed as enjoyable as having warm drinks while surrounded by blossoms. No decision came of our

---

55. It was customary to drink wine warm.

discussion. Then Yun laughed and said, "Come tomorrow, let each of you contribute a bit of money, and I'll bring the stove and fire." To which everyone laughed and said, "Very well."

After the group dispersed, I asked Yun, "Are you really going to bring everything yourself?"

She replied, "Not quite. I saw a vendor selling wontons in the market, fully equipped with pots and stoves. Why not hire him to come with us? I'll prepare everything beforehand and reheat it on the stove when we get there. This way we can have wine and tea both."

"That would certainly work for wine and dishes, but will we have anything to brew tea with?" I asked.

"I'll bring a clay pot," Yun replied, "and, with the wonton vendor's pot removed, hang the clay pot by an iron spike over the stove. Then we add firewood to brew the tea. Wouldn't that work?"

I had to applaud her cleverness. In the streets there was this wonton vendor by the name Bao. We hired him for a hundred coins, arranging for him to come the next afternoon, and he readily agreed. The next day, when our group of flower viewers arrived, I relayed Yun's idea, which was much admired by all.

After lunch, we all departed together for the South Garden with our mats. We chose a spot under the shade of willows and sat in a circle. We brewed tea first in order. Once done sipping, we warmed the wine and heated up the dishes.

The breeze was gentle in the brilliance of the sun, and the fields looked as if they were covered in gold, with shirts and dresses in blue and red crisscrossing therein, and butterflies and bees flitting about. The sight left us intoxicated without the help of any liquor.

When after a while, the wine had been warmed and dishes ready, we sat down again, indulging fully in the feast. The wonton vendor was quite the agreeable person, and we invited him to drink with us. Those walking by all envied our whimsical idea.

By the end, only empty cups and plates scattered around. All of us were left without a care, sitting or lying down, singing, whistling. As the crimson sun was about to fade, I began to crave porridge. The vendor went to get rice and made some for us, and we all went home with stuffed bellies.

"Did you all have a great excursion today?" Yun asked.

"We certainly would not have enjoyed it as much, had it not been for Madam's greatness!" they replied in unison. Then merrily we parted ways.

趣

A poor scholar's approach to his attire, daily necessities, and utensils should be one of economy but also of elegance. The principle of such economy is to "take things as they are."

For instance, I enjoy light libations and prefer to have only a few dishes. Yun designed a plum blossom dining set for me with six deep dishes of white porcelain, each two inches wide. One would be placed in the center, the other five arranged around it, painted with gray lacquer. The whole thus resembled a plum blossom. Both the base tray and the lid were beveled, and the lid was complete with a handle on top just like a flower stem.

When placed on the table, the set would look like a resting dark plum blossom. Opening the lid would reveal the dishes within the petals, with six compartments all in different colors, perfect for a gathering of two or three close friends, who could take what they liked and refill as needed.

Yun also made a round plate with low edges to hold our cups, chopsticks, and wine jugs, so that dinner could be served anywhere we pleased and be just as easily cleaned up. This is the principle of economy in food.

Yun also made all my caps, collars, and socks. Worn out clothes were patched from old clothes, but always kept tidy and clean. We wore muted colors so that stains would not be as conspicuous, and the colors were also fit for most occasions, be it at home or in travels. This reflects the economy in clothing.

When we first moved to the Free and Easy House, I found its interior too dark. We thus covered the walls with white paper, and the chambers brightened up instantly. And in the summertime, when the windows were removed, we felt the space looked too empty and exposed.

"There are some old bamboo curtains here. Why don't we use one of those in lieu of a screen?" Yun suggested.

"But how?" I asked.

"We can take several bamboo poles, paint them pitch-black, and crisscross them into a frame, just large enough for there to be still room below to walk through," she replied. "Then we can cut one of those curtains in half, about the height of the table, to hang on the horizontal pole, letting it drape to the ground.

"Then place four shorter bamboo poles vertically in the center and fasten them in place with hemp strings. We can find some black strips of fabric and sew them together to wrap up these poles and the horizontal pole. It would give us some privacy and look quite attractive without costing us much."

This is another application of "take things where they are." Seen this way, the belief of antiquity that "every part of bamboo and wood has its use" indeed has merit.

In the early summer season, when the lotus flowers first started to bloom, they would close at dusk and open again at dawn.

Yun would pack a few tea leaves in a small gauze pouch and place it in the heart of the flower. Upon being retrieved the next morning, she would brew the tea leaves in spring water. The fragrance, thus infused, was without parallel.

RECORD OF TRYING SORROW

Whence come the misfortunes of life? Often, these are retributions for one's own sins, but not so in my case.

I feel deeply. I keep my word. I speak my mind, and heed my heart. But for these I eventually suffered.

My father, Sir Jiafu, too, was generous and chivalrous, always eager to solve others' problems, to facilitate others' matters, to marry off friends' daughters, and to raise old friends' children. Such instances were too numerous to count. If he ever spent lavishly, it was mostly for the benefit of others.

From time to time, when my wife and I were short on money, we inevitably had to pawn some of our belongings. At the beginning, we would cut one hole to patch another, but overtime our means stretched ever thinner. As the proverb says, "Money matters in family matters." Our circumstances first drew the gossip of some petty people, and gradually the ridicule of others in the family. "Lack of talent is virtue in a woman" is truly an adage for the ages.

Although I am the eldest son, I was the third-born in the family. Hence, everybody used to call Yun "Third Lady." But at some point they started calling her "Third Wife" instead, a joke that eventually turned into habit. Everyone in the family, regardless of rank and age, all referred to her as the "Third Wife." Did this perhaps mark the beginning of the family's vicissitudes?

In the year Yi Si[56] during Emperor Qianlong's reign, I accompanied my father to the Haining court to serve him. Yun attached a small note in my mother's letter. My father saw it and said, "Since your wife can write, let's entrust your mother's letters to her."

Later, there was some chatter within the family, leading my mother

---

56. 1785.

to suspect that Yun did not relay affairs properly in the letters, so she stopped having Yun scribe them. Seeing the letters were no longer in Yun's handwriting, my father asked me, "Is your wife sick?" I thus inquired in a note to her but received no reply. Over time, my father grew offended, "I reckon your wife is too proud to take up the pen!"

Upon learning the real reason at home, I wanted to explain the matter to my father. But Yun was quick to stop me: "I'd rather take the blame from my father-in-law than lose favor with my mother-in-law!" And she never explained herself.

In the spring of Geng Cheng,[57] I again accompanied my father, this time to the Hanjiang court. There was a colleague of his by the name of Yu Futing, who had brought his family to live there. One time my father said to Futing:

"I have toiled my entire life, often living among strangers. I have long sought someone to attend to my everyday needs, but nothing has come of the effort. If our children could truly understand my feelings, they would find someone from my hometown, who could understand my native tongue."

Futing passed this message to me, and I sent a letter to Yun in secret, asking her to look for someone suitable. She found a young woman from the Yao family but did not immediately inform my mother of the matter, as it was still uncertain whether this match would succeed.

The woman arrived under the pretense of a neighbor's daughter visiting Hanjiang for leisure. But when I brought her to my father's residence at his behest, Yun took someone's advice and claimed that Yao was the woman my father had had in mind for a while. Upon seeing the woman, my mother remarked, "Isn't this the neighbor's daughter who only came here for a visit? Why should he marry her?" And so Yun lost favor with her mother-in-law as well.

---

57. 1790.

In the year of Ren Zi,[58] I took up residence at the Zhenzhou court. My father subsequently fell ill, with me following suit when I went to visit him in Hanjiang. My younger brother, Qitang, was with my father as well in Hanjiang at the time. While I was there, I received a letter from Yun:

Qitang borrowed money from a neighbor's wife and asked me to act as a guarantor. Now the creditor is pressing for repayment.

I asked Qitang about this, and he instead accused his sister-in-law of meddling with his affairs. I then wrote a reply, adding at the end:

Both father and son are ill. There is no money to repay the debt. When my younger brother returns, he can settle it himself.

Soon after, my father and I both recovered from our ailments. I left for Zhenzhou again, but Yun still wrote back to Hanjiang. My father opened the letter, which again mentioned the neighbor's loan to Qitang. The letter also read:

Your mother thinks the old man's ailment was all due to that concubine Yao. Now that father-in-law's condition has improved, it is best that we privately ask Yao to leave under the pretext of homesickness. I will arrange for her parents to fetch her in Yangzhou. I think this is the way for both sides to absolve themselves of any blame.

My father was enraged by the letter. He questioned Qitang about the matter with the neighbor, and Qitang claimed to know nothing about it. My father then wrote a stern letter to me, saying:

---

58. 1792.

Your wife borrowed money behind your back and slandered your younger brother for it. She refers to her mother-in-law as "your mother" and to her father-in-law as "the old man." This is truly preposterous! I have already sent someone to Suzhou to serve her with a letter of divorce. If you have any sense, you should recognize your blame.

When I received this letter, it felt like a thunderclap out of a clear sky. I immediately wrote a letter of contrition, mounted my horse, and rushed back home, worried that Yun might attempt to take her own life.

Hardly had I explained the situation when the family received the letter of divorce, which denounced Yun's actions in a tone both harsh and final. Yun cried, saying, "Of course I shouldn't have been so careless with my words, but father ought to forgive a woman's ignorance."

A few more days later, my father sent another directive:

I should not be too harsh on you. You shall take up residence elsewhere with your wife, out of my sight. This will spare me from further anger.

I thus began making arrangements for Yun to stay at her maternal family's home. However, since her mother had passed away and her younger brother was nowhere to be found, Yun was unwilling to live among her relatives. Fortunately, my friend Lu Banfan took pity on our predicament and invited the two of us to live in his residence, known as the Free and Easy House.

It was not until two years later that my father was apprised of the full story and paid a personal visit to the Free and Easy House, as I had just returned from Lingnan.

"I already know everything about what happened," my father said to Yun. "Would you come back home to live with us again?"

Thus delighted, we husband and wife returned to our old home, reunited again with our closest kin. But who could have foreseen the scourge that was Hanyuan!

Yun had long suffered from a blood illness due to her grief of her brother, who had left home and never returned, and her mother, Madam Jin, who had passed away, stricken by the loss of her son. After meeting Hanyuan, Yun went on for over a year without relapsing again, and I was overjoyed in thinking that she might have finally found her medicine.

However, Hanyuan was forced into marriage by some rich bully, who offered a thousand golds as a gift of betrothal and promised to look after her mother. The beauty now belonged to a browbeater! I knew of this but dared not tell Yun of it.

When Yun inquired about and learned of the truth, she returned, whimpering with sobs, and said to me, "I never expected that Hanyuan could be so heartless!"

"You were too blinded by your feelings," I replied. "What genuine feeling could there be in such people? Besides, those accustomed to brocade garments and jade meals will not rest content with a humble life of thorn hairpins and coarse skirts. It's better to have it fall through now than to have regrets later."

I consoled her thus over and over, but Yun remained woeful over the betrayal through to the end. Her blood illness relapsed, leaving her languishing in her bed. All treatments were ineffectual, and as bouts of illness came and went, her body became frail to the bone.

Within a few years, our debts piled up, and gossip in the family turned into grievances. My parents also increasingly detested her on account of her sworn sisterhood with a courtesan, and I had to mediate in the midst. It was no way to live.

Yun had given birth to a daughter named Qingjun, who was fourteen at the time. She was very well-mannered as well as capable, and we were grateful that she could work hard in such affairs as pawning our jewelry and garments. We also had a son named Fengsen, who was twelve at the time and learning to read under a tutor.

For several years I was in want of proper employment and had instead set up within our own home a small calligraphy and painting shop, whence three days' of income barely covered a single day's expense. I was worn out, and money was always short. In the depth of winter, I had to go out braving the cold, not having any fur coats, and Qingjun would shiver in her thin clothing yet still claim stubbornly, "It's not cold." For this reason Yun swore not to get any more treatment.

Once when she happened to be able to get out of bed, an old friend of mine, Zhou Chunxu, who had just returned from the court of the Duke of Fu, was looking for someone to embroider a copy of the *Heart Sutra*. Thinking that embroidering the sutra could dispel misfortunes and bring blessings, and moreover, that the embroidery would fetch a good price, Yun actually went ahead and embroidered it. Chunxu was in a hurry to depart and could not wait long, so Yun rushed to finish the work within ten days.

The intense labor further strained Yun, who was already frail, and exacerbated her backache and dizziness immediately. How could she have known that the ill-fated were beyond the mercy of the Buddha! After the embroidery work further aggravated her illness, those above and below in rank alike started detesting her for constantly asking for water or broth.

At the time, a Westerner had rented a house to the left of my art shop and made a living from usury. He often asked me to paint for him, and it was through this that I came to know him. A certain friend borrowed fifty golds from him and begged me to act as a guarantor. Finding the request hard to refuse on account of our friendship, I agreed.

However, this friend ran far away with the money and disappeared. The Westerner came to me, the guarantor, for repayment. At first, he accepted books and paintings as collateral, but eventually we had nothing left to offer.

At the end of the year, my father was at home when the Westerner came to demand repayment, howling outside our door. Hearing this, my father summoned me and chastised me, "How did we, a scholarly family, fall indebted to a lowly petty sort like him?!"

As I was trying to explain the matter, a visitor happened to turn up with inquiries for Yun's health at the behest of Yun's childhood sworn sister, a Madam Hua from Xishan, who had learned of Yun's illness. My father, mistaking her as a messenger from Hanyuan, grew even more enraged.

"Your wife does not abide by the proper conduct of the inner chambers, pledging sisterhood with a prostitute. You, too, fail to cultivate yourself, instead associating with petty sorts at will. I haven't the heart to push you off a cliff. I will give you three days to make up your mind about what course of action to take. After that, I shall take action against you in court for filial impiety!"

Hearing this, Yun wept, saying, "It is all because of my wrongdoing that father is so enraged. If I die and you go free, you certainly won't be able to bear it. If I stay, you leave, you will certainly regret leaving all this behind. Let's quietly call for the messenger from the Huas'. I will try to get up and make inquiries." She then had Qingjun help her outside the room and called for the messenger.

"Did your mistress purposefully send you here? Or did you come here on your way somewhere else?" Yun asked.

"The mistress had heard of your illness some time ago, Madam, and wanted to visit in person herself. But having never set foot in this door before, she dared not impose herself," the messenger replied. "Before dispatching me here, she instructed me to relay to you, 'If you wouldn't mind our humble village dwelling, you are more than welcome to convalesce there in the countryside. This would fulfill the promise we made under the lamp in our childhood.'"

It turned out that Yun and Madam Hua used to embroider together and once made a vow to support each other through sickness. Yun thus instructed the messenger, "If you would be so good to return quickly and ask your mistress to please send a boat, discreetly, in two days' time."

Once the person had left, Yun said to me, "My bond with my sworn sister Madam Hua is closer than that of flesh and blood. If you are willing to stay in her home, we might as well go together. Only that it would be inconvenient to bring the children along, nor would it be appropriate to leave them here and burden our parents. We must make proper arrangements within two days."

It happened so that I had a cousin, Wang Jinchen, who wished to marry Qingjun to his son, named Yunshi.

"I have heard," mused Yun, "that the Wang boy is weak and incapable, a son for keeping up the family's fortune at best, but his family has not much fortune to keep. However, he does come from a respectable family and is the only son. I think it is acceptable that we promise Qingjun to him."

I hence told Jinchen, "My father and you share the bond of uncle and nephew. If you wish to take Qingjun as your daughter-in-law, I reckon he'd have no objection. But if you wish to postpone the marriage until Qingjun is brought up, I'm afraid our circumstances would not allow it. After my wife and I leave for Xishan, you may ask my parents for permission to adopt Qingjun as a child daughter-in-law. How does that sound?" Jinchen was overjoyed and said, "I shall follow your instructions." Meanwhile we entrusted Fengsen to a friend,

Xia Yishan, who recommended him as an apprentice to a merchant.

No later than all these arrangements were made that the boat sent by the Huas arrived. This was the twenty-fifth day of the twelfth month, in the year of Geng Shen.[59]

"Us leaving home alone like this would draw the derision of neighbors," Yun contemplated. "Besides, we have not come up with the repayment to the Westerner, and I fear he would not let us pass. We must quietly depart early before dawn."

"Your illness is still in full swing," I said. "Will you be able to withstand the morning cold?"

"Death and life are governed by fate. Let's not worry needlessly," replied Yun.

I apprised my father of this plan in secret, and he also approved. That night, we first carried half a shoulder pole's worth of our belongings to the boat and put Fengsen to bed, while Qingjun sobbed at the side of her mother. Yun told her, "Your mother, so ill with fate and sick with love, is forced into displacement on that account. But thankfully your father is always good to me, so you have nothing to worry about. Within two or three years, our family shall reunite again.

"After you arrive at your new home," she continued, "abide by the feminine virtues—don't be like your mother. Your father- and mother-in-law feel very lucky to have secured this marriage and will certainly treat you well. Pray take all the belongings we are leaving behind with you.

"Your brother is still young, so we have not told him. At the time of parting, we are going to say that mother is traveling to see a doctor and will return in just a few days. You may explain the whole thing to him once we have traveled far and let your grandfather know we have left."

There was also an old lady—the same one from the foregoing chapter whose house we rented that one summer—who, having

---

59. 1800.

offered to accompany us to the countryside, was by our side at the time and who could not help wiping her tears.

With dawn soon approaching, we warmed some congee and ate it together. Yun forced a smile and said, "The family came together over congee, and will soon be dispersed over it, too. If one is to write a novella out of this, it may be titled *Romance of the Congee*."

Having heard us stirring about, Fengsen got up as well, whimpering, "What are you doing, mother?"

"I'm about to go see a doctor," Yun replied.

"But why so early?" Fengsen asked.

"Because we have a long way to travel," Yun said. "You stay home with your sister and don't bother grandmother. I'll be going with your father and coming back in just a few days."

Three rooster crows later, Yun, teary-eyed and supported by the old lady, was about to go out the backdoor when Fengsen suddenly broke out crying, "Waah!—my mother is not coming back!"

Qingjun covered Fengsen's mouth lest he wake the others up, comforting him. At that moment, Yun and I felt as if our insides were torn into a thousand pieces and were unable to utter a word besides "Don't cry. Don't cry."

After Qingjun shut the door behind us, Yun was able to walk only a dozen steps before her strength failed her. I asked the old lady to carry the lamp while I carried Yun on my back, and we went on. As we were approaching the boat, we almost got detained by patrol. Thankfully the old lady pretended Yun was her sick daughter and I her son-in-law, and the boatmen, who all worked for the Huas, upon hearing the commotion, came to our aid and helped us onto the boat. It was not until after we unfastened the boat and went on our way that Yun burst out crying.

This departure also marked the separation of mother and son forever.

Madam Hua's husband, given name Dacheng, lived by Wuxi's East High Mountain in a house that looked out to it. He made a living farming land and was a simple and honest man. His wife, maiden name Xia, was the aforementioned elder sister to Yun by pledge.

It was not until early in the afternoon that we arrived at their house that day. Madam Hua had already been waiting by the door and, with her two smiling young daughters, came forward to greet us at the boat. Delighted to see Yun, she helped Yun ashore, treating her with the utmost hospitality. Women and children from the surrounding neighborhood also rushed into the house, crowding around Yun. Some inquired after her health, some expressed their sympathy, and they whispered to each other, filling the room with the sound of chatter.

Yun said to Madam Hua, "Today truly makes me feel like a fisherman chance-entering the Peach Blossom Spring!"[60]

Madam Hua replied, "Don't tease us, sister. We ignorant villagers get easily excited."

It was here that we spent the New Years in peace. In the mere twenty days between our arrival and the Lantern Festival, Yun had gradually regained enough strength to rise and walk. She went out to watch the dragon lanterns at the threshing field that night, and her spirit and countenance slowly began to recover some liveliness. I also felt relieved because of this and discussed with Yun in private:

"My staying here is not a long-term solution. I wish to go look for employment elsewhere, but have no funds to travel. What should I do?"

"I have been considering this as well," she replied. "Your brother-in-law, Fan Huilai, is serving as an accountant for the salt bureau in Jingjiang.

---

60. Reference to Tao Qian's famed fable about a fisherman's chance discovery of an ethereal utopia where the people lead an ideal existence in harmony with nature, unaware of the outside world.

Ten years ago, he borrowed ten golds from you. We did not have enough and I had to pawn my hairpin to scrape it together. Remember?"

"Ah, I had forgotten all about it!" I said.

"I heard that Jingjiang is not too far from here. Why don't you go there?" she said, and I did as she suggested.

It was quite warm on the day I set out, and I was sweltering even just in my velvet gown and serge undercoat. This was the sixteenth day of the first month, year Xin You.[61] That night, I stayed at an inn in Xishan, where I fell asleep under a rented quilt.

The next morning, I boarded a boat for Jiangyin. We were sailing upwind the entire time, and it was drizzling, too. By the time we reached the river mouth in Jiangyin that night, I had been chilled to the bone and so bought some liquor to stave off the cold, for which I emptied my purse. I dithered about all night, trying to decide whether to pawn my clothes to scrape together the remaining fare.

On the nineteenth, the north wind was even harsher, the snowfall heavier, amidst I could not hold back wretched tears. I calculated the amount needed for accommodation and boat fare and decided I could not waste any money on alcohol. Just as my body and heart both shivered with the cold, I suddenly saw an old mister, dressed in straw sandals and a felt hat, carrying a yellow bag. As he entered the shop, he looked at me and I thought he looked familiar from somewhere.

"Old mister, aren't you of the Cao name from Taizhou?" I asked.

"Yes," he answered. "If not for you, I'd be lying dead in a ditch by now! My little girl is doing well and still often mentions your virtue. I never expected to meet you here today. What are you biding here for?"

As it happened, whilst performing my official service in Taizhou I had indeed encountered a Cao, who was of humble birth. He had a beautiful daughter, who had by then been betrothed, but a local

---

61. 1801.

man of influence had rendered him indebted in a plot to snatch his daughter. This had led to a legal dispute, and my intervention had helped return the daughter to her original betrothed. Cao had subsequently volunteered his service to the court and kowtowed to me in gratitude. That was how I came to know him.

I told him of how I had encountered the snowstorm on my way to seek assistance from a relative, to which he replied, "Tomorrow when the weather clears, I will escort you along the way." He then took out some money to buy wine, treating me in the most ardent manner.

On the twentieth day, just as the first morning bell rang, I heard the ferryman's call to board at the river mouth and immediately jumped out of bed, calling for Cao to join me.

"No hurry," Cao said. "Better eat first before boarding the boat."

He then paid for my room and food, then took me out for a drink. As I had been delayed for several days, I was eager to cross the river and barely managed to force down two sesame cakes for a lack of appetite. Once on the boat, the river wind pierced like arrows, and my limbs trembled. Cao said, "I heard someone from Jiangyin hanged themselves in Jing, and his wife hired this boat to go there. We have to wait for the hire to arrive in order to cross."

So we waited, with me starving in the cold, and it was not until noon that we finally unfastened our boat. By the time we reached Jing, the evening mist had already closed in on us.

"Now there are two salt bureaus in Jing," said Cao. "Are you going to the one inside the city, or outside?"

I staggered behind him and replied, "I truly don't know which one it is."

"In that case, let's sojourn here for the night and go visit tomorrow," he said.

When we entered the inn, my socks and shoes had been soaked in mud. I asked for fire to dry them, had a hasty meal, and fell into an exhausted slumber. I got up in the morning to see that my socks had been burnt with just half of each remaining. Cao paid for my room and meals again.

When we got to the office in the city, Huilai had not risen. Hearing my arrival, he hurriedly put on his clothes to come meet me.

"Brother-in-law, how come you look so disheveled?" he said in disbelief.

"Pray don't make me tell," I said. "First, have you got two golds you could loan me, so I can pay back my escort?"

Huilai thus fetched two barbarian cakes[62] for me, which I offered to Cao. He insisted on not having them, finally accepting only one, and left.

I then recounted all that I had suffered and explained the purpose of my visit. Huilai said, "You and I are brothers by marriage. Even if there was no old debt, I still ought to do my utmost to help.

"Unfortunately, as our salt boat out at sea has just been taken by pirates, we are in the midst of straightening out the accounts, and I've got more funds I can move around. The best I could do is to give you twenty coins of barbarian silver to repay the old debt. How does that sound?"

I had no extravagant hopes to begin with and so agreed. I stayed on for two more days and, when the weather was again clear and warm, promptly made plans to return. I arrived back at Hua's residence on the twenty-fifth.

"Did you encounter the snow?" Yun asked me.

I then told her of my ordeal, to which she replied sorrowfully, "When it snowed, I thought you would have reached Jingjiang and did not expect you had to linger on at the river mouth. Thankfully you ran into that Mr. Cao. That miraculous opening when all seemed lost really is heavens' favor to the good."

---

62. Foreign coins.

Several days later, we received a letter from Qingjun and learned that Fengsen had been accepted as an apprentice at a shop by way of Yishan's recommendation, and further that Jinchen had obtained my father's permission to take Qingjun home on the twenty-fourth of the first month. Children's affairs were thus more or less settled, yet our separation still filled me with anguish.

The weather was lovely in the early second month. With the silvers I had obtained in Jingjiang, I packed up my luggage to visit an old friend, Hu Kentang, who was serving at the salt bureau in Hanjiang at the time. By way of his recommendation, I obtained a clerical position at the tax bureau, and I was finally able to feel more at ease both in mind and body.

The following year, in the eighth month of Ren Xu,[63] I received a letter from Yun:

My sickly body has recovered completely. I do not think it befits me to live indefinitely under the roof where the master is neither friend or family. I wish to join you in Hanjiang and admire the splendor of Level Mountain.

I hence rented a two-beam lodging facing the river, outside the Harbinger Spring Gate in Hanjiang, and went to the Huas' to fetch Yun myself. Madam Hua gifted us a little servant boy by the name of Ah-Shuang to help with the cooking. We also agreed that someday we would live as neighbors.

It was already the tenth month, and Level Mountain had turned cold and desolate, so we planned to visit the following spring instead.

---

63. 1802.

We were fully hoping that we would rest and recuperate here and eventually reunite with our family. Yet less than a month later, the tax bureau unexpectedly cut fifteen of its staff. As I was only the friend of a friend, I once more found myself idle.

At first, Yun was still racking her wit to draw up plans for me. She comforted me in spite of her own agitation and did not say a word of complaint. But by the second month of spring in Gui Hai, her blood illness relapsed severely. I wanted to go to Jingjiang again and call my brother-in-law for help, but Yun said, "Better to seek help from friends than from relatives."

"You are right enough there," I said. "But as much as our friends care for our well-being, they are also idling at home, unable to look after themselves, let alone us."

"Thankfully the weather has warmed by now, and you should not have to worry about being encumbered by snow," she said. "May your travels be smooth and speedy. Pray don't worry about me. If anything were to happen to you, that would only deepen my sin."

At the time we were already in a pinch, but in order to ease Yun's mind, I pretended to hire a mule, while in fact I set off on foot with only some bread, eating as I traveled southeast. I crossed two rivers on the way, and for eighty to ninety *li*, there was not even a hamlet in sight. By around eight o'clock in the evening, all I could see was the vast and lonely yellow sand and bright stars flickering in the night sky.

I then came upon a small shrine, about five feet high, surrounded by a low stone wall and two cypress trees. Kowtowing to the deity therein, I prayed, "I am Shen of Suzhou, and I have ended up here after losing my way on my travels to visit relatives. I wish to seek shelter for one night. Mayst thou pity and protect me."

I moved the small stone incense burner aside and tried squeezing myself in, but there was only room for half of my torso, so I turned my cap around to shield my face, sat with half of my body inside, and let my legs hang out. As I shut my eyes, I heard only the soft rustling of the wind. Feet tired, spirit fatigued, I swooned into a deep sleep.

When I woke up, the eastern sky had already whitened. I then heard footsteps approaching outside the wall and hurried out to see a group of local villagers passing the place by on their way to the market. I asked them for directions.

"Go south for ten *li*, and you will reach Taixing County. Go through the town and head southeast, and you will see a dirt mound every ten *li*. You will arrive at Jingjiang after eight of those. The roads are all wide and clear."

Turning around, I returned the incense burner to its original position and kowtowed again in thanks before going on my way. After passing Taixing, I was able to hitch a ride on a small cart. I arrived at Jingjiang at around four o'clock in the afternoon.

I sent in my card and waited for a long time before the guard told me, "Master Fan has gone to Changzhou on official business." From his tone, this seemed only a pretext. I thus pressed him, "When will he return?"

"I don't know," the guard replied.

"Then I shall wait for him to return, even if it means a year," I said.

The guard understood my intention and asked discreetly, "Are you Master Fan's bona fide brother-in-law?"

"If I were not, I wouldn't wait here for his return," I replied.

"Then please wait for him," he said.

Three days later, he informed me that Fan had returned to Jing, and I was able to borrow twenty-five golds.

I hired a mule and hurried home, only to find Yun sobbing in distress, looking as if some calamity had just happened. Seeing my return, she burst out, "Did you know that yesterday afternoon Ah-Shuang swept up our things and ran away? I have asked people to search everywhere, but they still haven't found him.

"Losing our things is a small matter," she continued, "but before we left, A-Shuang's mother had told me over and over for us to take good care of him. If he's running home, with the great river[64] blocking his path, I fear something awful might happen to him. And what if his parents should decide to hide him away in a plot to cheat us? What would we do then? And how could I face my sworn sister!"

"Pray calm down," I replied. "Your concern seems unfounded. Those who hide their children only cheat the wealthy, while you and I live from hand to mouth. Besides, since we brought him here half a year ago, we have given him clothing and shared our food with him, and have never beaten or even so much as scolded him. The neighbors all know this.

"The fact of the matter is that the little servant boy lost his conscience and took advantage of a moment of crisis to steal from us. Your sworn sister of the Hua family gave us a thief. If anything, it should be her who could not face you, so why should you say that you cannot face her? Now, we should report this to the county and file a case to prevent any future trouble."

Yun seemed somewhat relieved by these words, but thereafter she often talked in her dreams, crying out, "Ah-Shuang ran away!"—or "Why did Han betray me?"—and her illness deteriorated by the day.

I wished to call a doctor to treat her, but Yun stopped me, saying, "My illness was first started up by my grief when my brother vanished and my mother passed away, advanced by my fits of passion, and now aggravated by this bout of anger. To boot, I have always been prone to excessive worry.

"I tried so hard to be a good daughter-in-law but have failed, hence this dizziness in the head, these palpitations of the heart, and all the other symptoms of what they call being sick to the vitals. Even the best doctor would be of no avail. Pray do not waste money on futile expenses.

---

64. Yangtze River.

"I recall how, in these twenty-three years that I have followed you, I have had the honor of your loving affection and thoughtful consideration in spite of all my faults, and how you never once abandoned me for my waywardness. To have a husband who knows me as well as you too, I already have no regrets in this life.

"Besides, I've had clothes to keep me warm, meals to keep me fed, and a well-kept room to keep me sheltered; I have strolled among many fine springs and rocks; have had such fortunate circumstances as sojourns at the Pavilion of Azure Waves and the Free and Easy House. I have lived this earthly life like an immortal.

"Yet how many lifetimes of virtue does it take for one to attain that immortal state? And who are we to dare hope for such attainment? Having pursued happiness beyond our lot, we have offended the Creator, and with our passion we have incurred troubles onto ourselves—all because you love me too much, and because I am so ill-fated!"

At this she began weeping but continued: "Even a life of a hundred years ends in death. Now that we are parting in the middle of the journey, with a long separation suddenly ahead of us, I regret that I will not be able to fulfill my domestic duties to you through the end of life, nor will I see Fengsen marry. This truly pains my heart."

As she finished speaking, her tears were already falling like beads. I held back my own grief and tried to comfort her, "You've been ill for eight years and gone through many such dire moments. Why do you suddenly speak such heart-wrenching words today?"

"For many nights in a row I have dreamed of my parents sending a boat for me," she replied. "As soon as I close my eyes, I feel as if I were floating, now upward, now downward, moving through mists and clouds. Doesn't this mean my soul is already departing, leaving only this shell of a body behind?"

"Your spirit has been disturbed," I said. "With nourishments and medicine, combined with rest, you will certainly regain your health."

Yun sighed deeply and said, "If I had so much as a glimmer of hope to live, I would never dare speak such things to you. But the end is near. If I do not speak now, there may be no other chance. You have lost the affection of your family, drifting from place to place, all because of me.

"Once I die, you'll regain your family's affection again and will no longer have to miss them from afar. Your parents are growing old, too. After my death, you should return to them quickly. If you can't bring my remains with you, you may leave them here temporarily, until a future time comes for you to collect them.

"May you find yourself someone beautiful and virtuous to remarry, to care for your parents and raise my son. Then I shall be at peace."

Having thus spoken, Yun looked as if her insides were torn to pieces and started bawling uncontrollably.

"If you really are leaving me in the middle of the journey, there is no reason why I should marry someone else," I said. "Besides, 'No water's enough when you have crossed the sea; no cloud is true but that which crowns the peak.'"[65]

Clutching my hands in hers, she seemed as if she had much more to say but could only utter the two words, "another life," over and over. Anon she grew short of breath and ceased speaking. Her eyes widened. No matter how hard I called out to her, she could not answer. Only two lines of sorrowful tears streamed down her face. And soon her breathing fell shallow. The tears dried. Her spirit seemed to drift away—and then departed this life forever.

This was the thirtieth of the third month, Gui Hai,[66] during the reign of Jiaqing. A lone lamp was my only company then. My family was nowhere to be seen, and my person was bare of possessions. My already shriveled heart was breaking into pieces, and the grief—it is everlasting, for how could it end?

---

65. Line by Yuan Zhen. "Cloud" is a homophone of Yun.
66. 1803.

愁

Courtesy of my friend Hu Shengtang's aid in the form of ten golds, and together with all the proceeds from my selling everything in the household, I buried Yun myself.

Alas! Yun was a woman with a man's magnanimity and intellect. After she married into my family, I had to run about endlessly to provide for the household, and still we never had enough, yet she never had a word of complaint. And when I was home, our only diversion consisted of discussion of books and literature. She died of illness and displacement, filled with regret unto the end. Who was to blame? I had failed my dearest companion in ways beyond words.

I would advise all the world's husbands and wives certainly not to harbor hatred towards each other, but not to fall passionately attached, either. As the saying goes, "A loving couple does not grow old together." My case may serve as a cautionary tale.

The Night of Spirits' Return is the time, according to common belief, when souls follow along evil spirits to return to this world. For this occasion, one would arrange the household as it was during the deceased's lifetime, and lay out the deceased's old clothes on the bed and place the deceased's old shoes beneath, so that the soul may return and see them. In Wu, this custom is known as "collecting the soul's gaze." A Taoist priest is sometimes called to perform a ritual, whereby the soul is first summoned to the bed and then sent away, known as "welcoming the ghost."

The custom of Hanjiang, however, is to set out drinks and dishes in the deceased's room, whence the entire family must leave in order to "avoid the ghost." There have been instances where a household is burglarized because of this.

When it was time for Yun to return, our landlord, who lived in the same house, went out. The neighbors advised me to set out offerings and get away as well. Hoping to catch a glimpse of Yun's returning soul, I only responded in vague agreement. My fellow townsman Zhang Yumen urged me, "Whoever comes in contact with evil spirits may well become possessed. In this case, it's better to believe in the existence of ghosts and spirits. Pray don't try your luck!"

"I am waiting here and not getting away precisely because I believe in ghosts," I replied.

"Encounters with those spirits do not bode well for the living," said Zhang. "Even if Madam's soul really returns, there will still be that gulf between life and death keeping you apart. I fear that the one you hope to see will not take shape, while the spirits you should avoid will be provoked."

But I, already obsessed, insisted, "Death and life are governed by fate. If you really care so much, how about accompanying me there?"

"I will stand guard outside the door," he replied. "In case of any abnormality, just call out to me, and I'll come in."

I then lit a lamp and went into the room. Seeing that the room was exactly as she had left it, but her voice and face were no more, I could not help bursting into tears. Worried that with blurred vision I would miss the chance to see her, I strained to hold the tears back and keep my eyes open as I sat on the bed, waiting.

I traced my fingers on her old clothes, where her fragrance still lingered, feeling so grief-stricken that I fell down in a swoon. But then I thought to myself, "How could I let myself doze off when I was waiting for her soul to return?"

I flicked my eyes open to see that the pair of candles on the mat glimmered with blue flames the mere size of peas. My flesh crept at the sight, shuddering all over. Rubbing my hands on my forehead, I sought to get a closer look, whence the two flames rose higher and higher until they were over one *chi* tall,[67] all but setting the paper-

---

67. About three feet.

framed ceiling ablaze. As I looked around the illuminated room, the light shrank again to its former size.

Heart pounding and legs trembling, I wanted to call for my guard to come in to see this, but on second thought feared that Yun's soul might be delicate and frail, easily threatened by a *yang* force. Instead I called Yun's name softly and prayed for her. The room was dead silent, with nothing to be seen. Thereafter the candlelight grew bright again but did not leap higher. I went out and told Yumen what had happened, and he was impressed by my valor. He did not know that I was merely beside myself with longing.

After Yun's death, I thought back to Hejing's adage, "take plum as wife, crane as son," and gave myself the literary name Meiyi.[68]

I had Yun buried outside the West Gate of Yangzhou, on Mount Gold Osmanthus, a place commonly known as the Hao Pagoda. I purchased a burial plot and, following her last words, placed her there for the time being. Afterward, I took Yun's spirit tablet back home. My mother also bemoaned her death, and Qingjun and Fengsen, having returned, cried bitterly as they went into mourning.

"Father's anger has not eased," Qitang told me. "It would be best for you to go back to Yangzhou for now. When father returns, I shall speak to him for you and write to you when it is time to come home."

I hence bade weeping farewell to my mother and children. After returning to Yangzhou, I sold paintings to make ends meet. There, I often found myself crying by Yun's grave, lonesome and desolate. On occasion I would pass by our old house, eyes seared and heart wounded by the sight.

On the Double Ninth Festival, all the neighboring grave mounds had turned yellow, but Yun's alone remained green. The gravekeeper told me, "This is a good burial place. The earth spirits are strong here."

---

68. Literally, plum free.

I thus prayed silently: "The autumn wind is closing in, but my clothes remain thin. If you have the power, may you bless me in my search for a post, so I can make it through the remainder of the year here as I await word from home."

Before long, Mr. Zhang Yu'an, who held a clerical post at the Jiangdu court, was heading back to Zhejiang to bury a parent and asked me to take his place for three months. I was thus able to purchase some warm clothing for the winter.

After I left that post, Zhang Yumen invited me to stay at his house for a while. Zhang, too, was out of employment and barely scraping by. He consulted me for his troubles, and I lent him all the twenty golds I had, saying, "I had reserved this for the purpose of taking my dead wife's coffin home. You may repay me once I receive word from home to return."

I spent the New Years that year at Zhang's, where I had waited day and night for news from home. None had come.

In the third month of Jia Zi,[69] I received a letter from Qingjun and learned that my father had fallen ill. I immediately thought about returning to Suzhou but was afraid that doing so might reanimate my father's old grievances. Just as I was dithering about, there came another letter from Qingjun, and that was when I learned my father had passed away.

Grief pierced me to the bone, and I could only cry out to the heavens in vain. Without further thought for anything else, I dashed back that very night, beneath the stars.

I knocked my head before his coffin until I bled, wailing bitterly. Alas! My father had toiled all his life, working tirelessly away from home, but had begotten such an unfilial son as I, who neither

---

69. 1804.

gladdened him in my younger years nor served him in his time of illness. How would I ever be resolved from so grievous a sin?

"Why have you only returned today?" my mother, seeing me cry, asked.

"I would not even have known to return today, had it not been the letter from Qingjun, your granddaughter," I replied. My mother cast a look at my brother and his wife, but kept silent.

Throughout the seven weeks I kept watch of my father's coffin in the hall, not a single person discussed family matters or funeral arrangements with me. For my part, I knew I had failed in my duties as a son and so was too ashamed to make inquiries.

One day a group of men turned up unexpectedly, clamoring at our door to demand repayment of a loan from me. I went out and responded:

"It is certainly within your right to demand repayment of defaulting debts. But taking the occasion of another's misfortune to advance your pursuit, when my father's body has scarcely gone cold, is surely going too far!"

At this, one of them pulled me aside and said, "We are merely acting at someone else's behest. If you step away, we will go to the person who called us here to seek repayment from him directly."

"If I owe a debt, I'll certainly repay it. Pray leave this instant!" I said, and they all left meekly.

I then called for Qitang and told him: "I may be an unfilial son, but I have never committed any evil or wrongdoing. When I was named heir to father's deceased cousin, I did not claim even a morsel of inheritance. Do you suppose I returned home this time to fight over the estate, rather than to fulfill my duties as a son in mourning? A man's dignity lies in standing on his own two feet. I came back with nothing, and I shall leave with nothing!"

Having thus spoken, I turned back into the mourning hall, where I became overcome with my feelings and gave in to sobs.

I then kowtowed farewell to my mother and went to tell Qingjun that I was to leave at once and retreat deep into the mountains, where I would seek out the immortal Chisongzi[70] away from the mundane world. Just as Qingjun was trying to dissuade me, my friends, Xia Nanxun, courtesy name Dan'an, and Xia Fengtai, courtesy name Yishan, arrived having learned of my whereabouts.

The two brothers urged me vehemently, "Your anger and vexation are understandable given your family circumstances. Yet though your father has passed, your mother is still living; though your wife is dead, your son is not yet grown. How could you be at peace with drifting away from the world?"

"What other resort have I then?"

"You could put up in our humble abode for the time being," Dan'an said, "I heard that His Excellency Shi Zhuotang has written to say that he is coming home on leave. Why not wait for his return and pay a visit? He will certainly have a position in mind for you."

"I'm still in my hundred days of mourning, and you two have elderly parents at home. I fear this might be inappropriate," I said.

"This humble invitation from us also extends our father's wish," Yishan replied. "If you feel it is inconvenient, there is also a Chan[71] temple nearby, and the abbot is a close friend of mine. If you are so inclined, you may stay at the temple. How does that sound?"

To this I agreed. Qingjun then added, "The property grandfather left behind is worth at least three or four thousand golds. Seeing you have already declined to take any share of it, will you really relinquish your own belongings as well? I shall retrieve it and bring it directly to the temple father will be staying at."

And thanks to Qingjun, not only did I recover my belongings,

---

70. Literally, Master Red Pine; Chinese rain god.
71. School of Buddhism that originated in China and further developed in the rest of East Asia, including Japan, where it is known as Zen.

I also got possession of several other items—books, inkstones and brush holders—my father had left behind.

The monks at the temple put me up in the Hall of Great Compassion. The hall faced south, and to its east was a statue of some deity. I occupied the westmost room, which, being the place where the Buddhists would eat their observant meals, had a moon window directly across from the Buddha niche. By the door there stood a most imposing statue of Warrior Saint Guan holding a broadsword.

In the courtyard, there was a ginkgo tree, three embraces in circumference, with a shade large enough to cover the entire pavilion. The wind would blow through its branches like roars in the otherwise quiet night. Yishan, who often brought wine and fruit to drink with me, once asked me, "Staying alone here and often staying up at night, do you not feel fear?"

"I have lived my life with a clear conscience, with no evil desires. What's to fear?" I replied.

Not long after I had settled there, there was a torrential downpour, which continued day and night for thirty consecutive days. I was at times worried that the ginkgo tree's branches might snap and break the roof. But divine protection kept us all safe, though many buildings outside the temple did collapse, and nearby rice fields were flooded, the stalks therein washed away. As for me, I spent my days painting with the monks in a state of oblivion.

At the beginning of the seventh month, the sky finally cleared. Yishan's father, styled Chunxiang, was going to Chongming for some business dealings and invited me to accompany him as a personal scribe. From this I earned twenty golds.

Upon returning home, I found that my father's burial was imminent. For this Qitang sent Fengsen, who told me, "Uncle is short of funds for the funeral and would like a contribution of ten or twenty golds." I had planned to give him all I had, but Yishan would not allow it, insisting that I only contribute half the amount. I then went ahead to the grave site with Qingjun.

After the burial, I returned to the Pavilion of Great Compassion. At the end of the ninth month, Yishan, who owned some farmland by the East Sea near Yongtai Sands, invited me to accompany him to collect rents. We stayed for two months, and by the time we returned, winter had already set in. We moved into his home, Snow-and-Wild-Goose Cottage, to spend the New Years. He was my kin by a different surname indeed.

In the seventh month of Yi Chou,[72] Zhuotang finally came home from the capital. His given name was Yunyu, courtesy name Zhiru, and Zhuotang was his style name. He and I were childhood chums. In Geng Xu during Qianlong's reign,[73] Zhuotang took first place in the imperial examinations and was thereafter appointed Prefect of Chongqing, Sichuan. During the White Lotus Rebellion, he attained remarkable feats in the campaigns against rebels.

The reunion gladdened us both. Shortly after, on the Double Ninth, he was to return to his post in Chongqing with his family and invited me to accompany him. I thus bade farewell to my mother for the fourth time, at the home of Lu Shangwu, my ninth sister's husband, as our ancestral home now already belonged to someone else.

"Your brother is not to be relied upon, you must make your best endeavors on this trip," my mother instructed. "The revival of our family reputation depends entirely on you!"

As for Fengsun, he saw me off half of the way but then started sobbing uncontrollably, so I bade him go home.

When the boat passed by Jingkou, Zhuotang decided he wanted

---

72. 1805.
73. 1790.

to visit his old friend Wang Tifu, a second degree holder[74] serving at the Huaiyang Salt Bureau, and so we took a detour. I hence also got another chance to visit Yun's grave.

After embarking again, we went up the Yangtze River, taking in famous scenery along the way. Upon arriving in Jingzhou in Hubei, we learned that Zhuotang had been promoted to Inspectorate of Tongguan. He thus asked me to stay in Jingzhou with his son, Dunfu, and the rest of his family for the time being, while he traveled on light with a reduced retinue to Chongqing to spend the New Years. Thence he would move on to his new post from Chengdu via the cliff roads.

In the second month of Bing Yin,[75] the rest of the family and I also continued on, first traveling by water to reach Fancheng, where we went ashore. The ensuing land route was long, the expenses burdensome, the carriages heavy with luggage and riders, with horses dying and cartwheels breaking along this torturesome journey.

Just three months after we had finally reached Tongguan, Zhuotang was promoted again, this time to Provincial Judge in Shanzuo.[76] Being an honest and upright public servant who never unjustly enriched himself, Zhuotang did not have the funds to pay his family to accompany him. We thus temporarily stayed at Tong River Academy.

It was not until the end of the tenth month that Zhuotang received his salary and sent someone to fetch his family. The messenger also brought a letter for me. It was from Qingjun. From the letter I learned the harrowing news that Fengsen had died in April. I recalled the day when he had cried as he sent me off—it ended up being a father and son's eternal parting. Alas! He was Yun's only son, and now there would be no heir to carry on her ancestral line.

---

74. A title bestowed upon those who succeeded in the provincial civil service examinations.
75. 1806.
76. Now Shandong Province.

Zhuotang, upon hearing this news, also sighed deeply. He subsequently gifted me a concubine, ushering me back into the spring dream of life. From that point on it was all sound and fury, a dream whence I do not know when I shall wake.

RECORD OF MERRY WAYFARING

    In the thirty years of my moving from post to official post, I have practically traveled everywhere in the country, with the only provinces I have yet to visit being Sichuan, Guizhou, and Yunnan.

    Unfortunately, the nature of official travel is such that the wheel and hoof have always been in quick succession, with me being part of only some procession, and those soul-enriching sceneries of landscape have often passed before my eyes like ephemeral clouds, without me having the opportunity to fully take stock of their grandeur or explore the secluded corners therein.

    I prefer to form my own opinions on everything and disdain to follow the judgments of others. In poetry and painting, for instance, I am not afraid to dismiss what others prize highly and prize highly what others dismiss. Likewise, when it comes to famous sceneries, I feel what truly matters is the feeling one derives from them. There are therefore renowned scenic sights I fail to find impressive, and other lesser-known ones that I believe to be rather marvelous. Here I only record the places as I have experienced them.

    When I was fifteen years old, my father, Sir Jiafu, was employed by a Magistrate Zhao Ming in Shanyin. There was an esteemed scholar Master Zhao Shengzhai, given name Chuan, from Hangzhou, whom Magistrate Zhao had invited to tutor his own son, and I studied under him as well per my father's instruction.

    On a day with no lessons, I went on an excursion to Howling Mountain about ten *li* from the city, unreachable by land routes. As we approached the mountain, we saw a cave, with a slab of rock above cracked horizontally and looking as if it was about to fall.

    We rowed our boat into the cave from beneath the slab, and our view suddenly opened up to a capacious interior enclosed by steep walls on all sides, commonly known as the "water garden." By the water there stood a stone pavilion of five beams, and on the opposite wall across there was the inscription, *Behold the leaping fish*. The water was unfathomably deep, and legend had it that a giant fish lurked therein. I threw out some bait tentatively, only to attract some nibblers less than a *chi* long.

Behind the pavilion, there was a passage leading to the "dry garden," where the rockery only consisted of a mingle-mangle of rocks. Some of these were only wide as a palm, and some pillars were capped evenly on top for bigger rocks to attach, with visible chisel marks, all in all quite unattractive.

After touring the place, we picnicked in the pavilion by the water and had the accompanying servant set off some firecrackers. Loud booms went off like claps of thunder, reverberating through all the nearby mountains. This was the beginning of my carefree roaming, dating back to my younger years, only to this day I still regret that I have never visited the Orchid Pavilion or the Tomb of Emperor Yu.

The year after my arrival in Shanyin, my teacher set up a study in his own home on the consideration that he should not be far away from home with now aging parents. I thus followed him to Hangzhou, where I was able to enjoy the magnificence of West Lake.

In terms of their structural intricacies, I think Dragon Well the most exquisite, with Heaven's Garden second. The best rocks can be found at the Peak that Flew Hither in Tianzhu, or in the Ancient Cave of Auspicious Stones on the City God's Hill. Jade Spring has the best water, clear and lively with a plentitude of fish. The worst is perhaps the Agate Temple of Ge Ridge. The rest, such as the Mid-Lake Pavilion and the Six Ones Spring,[77] each has its own merits, which I shall not go into detail to describe here, except that none is free of an overly made-up effect. Over these I rather favor the seclusion of the Studio of Tranquility, whose elegance derived from its air of naturalness.

---

77. After Ouyang Xiu, who referred to himself as Hermit Six Ones in his later years.

The tomb of Su Xiao is situated by the West Burble Bridge, which by the natives' account was a small mound of yellow dirt when first discovered. However, in the year of Geng Zi during Qianlong's reign,[78] His Majesty visited the place on his Southern Inspection Tour and inquired about it. By His Majesty's next Southern Inspection Tour during spring of Jia Chen,[79] Su Xiao's tomb had been laid with stones into an octagon. A large stone tablet atop bears the inscription, *The Tomb of Su Xiao of Qiantang*.[80] From then on, poets and literati in search of a bygone memory need no longer wander around looking for it.

I could not help but reflect on how, since antiquity, countless heroic spirits and loyal souls have been buried unrecorded, and how even most of those remembered have faded back into oblivion after a short while. Yet Su Xiao, a mere courtesan, has since the Southern Qi period been known by all, perhaps because she was blessed with an ethereal essence which now graces the lakes and mountains?

A few steps north of the bridge is the Chongwen Academy, where I once took examinations with my fellow student Zhao Jizhi. It was a long summer day, and we rose very early. We went out the Qiantang Gate, passed by Zhaoqing Temple, and ascended the Broken Bridge, where we sat down on the stone balustrade. The sun was just about to rise, and the morning glow was reflected in the water outside the willows in a most exquisite way. The fragrance of white lotus flowers filled the air, and the occasional gentle breeze refreshed one to the heart and bone. When we walked thence to the academy, the exam questions had not yet been handed out.

I submitted my exam papers early in the afternoon, and then went with Jizhi to enjoy the cool air in the Cave of Purple Clouds. The cave was large enough for several dozen people, with sunlight spilling in

---

78. 1780.
79. 1784.
80. Qiantang: Another name for Hangzhou.

shafts through the openings above. A wine vendor had set up a small table and low stools here, so we took off our gowns and had a little to drink. We also had some dried venison, which was quite delicious, with fresh water chestnuts and white lotus root as sides.

We left the cave slightly intoxicated. Jizhi suggested, "Sunrise Terrace is right above us, and its height allows an open view. Why don't we go there for a visit?"

I was also in the mood. We climbed to the top with great fervor, and looking down from the summit, I thought West Lake resembled a mirror, the city of Hangzhou a small pellet, and the Qiantang River a ribbon. The view extended as far as the eye could see for several hundred *li*. This was the grandest view I have seen in this life.

We sat there for a long time and only descended the mountain together when the sun was about to set and the evening bell of South Screen Temple had begun to toll. We did not make it to Taoguang and Yunqi as they were farther away. The other sights, such as the plum blossoms at Red Gate Bureau or the iron tree at the Nuns' Temple, were rather unremarkable.

I had believed the Cave of Purple Sun to be something worth seeing, but when we finally visited, I saw that the entrance could barely fit one finger, with only a trickle of water flowing through it. It is said that there is a world of its own inside the cave, and I regret that we could not pry it open to enter.

On Tomb-Sweeping Day, my teacher went to visit his ancestral grave, located in the bamboo-rich East Mountain, and brought me along. The gravekeeper offered us some soup made from bamboo shoots he had dug up before they had come above ground. Sharp at the tip, they resembled pears in shape. I found them delectable and savored two full bowls of the soup.

"Alas! As delicious as these are, they wear on one's heart and blood. You should eat more meat to counter the effect," my teacher said.

I never had much of a penchant for butchered fare and also found my appetite for rice also reduced because of the bamboo shoots. On our way back, I felt irritably parched, my lips and tongue all but cracking. We passed by Stone House Cave, which was not particularly remarkable. The Cave of Water Joy, on the other hand, had steep cliffs covered by thick wisteria vines. We entered the cave to see a spring gushing and gurgling in its attic-sized interior, with a pool underneath only about three *chi* wide and five *cun* deep, neither ebbing nor overflowing. I bent down to drink therein, and my thirst was immediately quenched.

Outside this cave there were two small pavilions, whence one could hear the sound of the spring. By some monks' invitation, we also got to see the Ten Thousand Years' Urn, which was of enormous size and placed in the kitchen of the Temple of Stored Fragrance. A bamboo pipe channeled water from the spring into the urn, and one could hear the water bubbling therein. Over the years, a layer of moss, perhaps over one *chi* thick, has covered its surface. For this reason the urn never froze in the winter and was able to stay intact.

The autumn of Xin Chou,[81] in the eighth month, my father returned home after falling ill to malaria. He would call for fire when cold, and for ice when feverish, despite me advising him to the contrary. The illness eventually turned into a case of typhoid, which deteriorated by the day. I attended to his medicine and care day and night with no proper sleep for nearly a month. My wife Yun was also seriously sick at the time, enfeebled and bedridden. All this left me in a foul, indescribably bleak mood.

"I am afraid I won't recover from this illness," my father called me to his bedside one day and instructed, thinking these were his final

---

81. 1781.

words. "You may have read a few books, but you won't be able to make a living for yourself from that. I shall entrust you to my sworn brother, Jiang Sizhai, so that you may continue my profession."

The next day, Sizhai came over and I kowtowed to him as my teacher by my father's bedside. However, not long after, my father was treated by a renowned doctor, Master Xu Guanlian, and gradually recovered his health thereafter. Yun was also able to regain enough strength to get out of bed thanks to Dr. Xu's treatment. As for me, from that point on, I began to learn the clerical profession from Master Sizhai.

This is no merry story, so why record it in this chapter? To this I answer: here lies the beginning of my abandoning books and aimlessly wandering, and thus, it is worth recording.

That winter, I followed Master Sizhai, given name Xiang, to Fengxian Palace for my clerical studies. Among my fellow students of the profession was Gu Jinjian, courtesy name Honggan, style name Zixia, also from Suzhou. He was a fellow of generosity and fortitude, upright and never fawning, and was one year older than me, so I addressed him as "big brother." Honggan, in turn, took me as his "little brother" and we became fast friends.

Honggan was my first true bosom friend, but regrettably, he passed away at the age of twenty-two. After that, I grew withdrawn, and now, at the age of forty-six, adrift in the vast sea of existence, I do not know whether I will ever meet a friend like Honggan again in this life.

I recall when I first made my friendship with Honggan, our hearts were expansive, and our minds were lofty, filled with ideas like retreating one day to a secluded life in the mountains.

On the Double Ninth, Honggan and I both found ourselves in Suzhou. My father, Sir Jiafu, and his friend Wang Xiaoxia, had invited some actresses to entertain guests at our home with some theatrical performances that day. I was not fond of the noise and furor of such affairs and so had arranged, a day in advance, with Honggan to visit Cold Mountain for a hike as well as the double purpose of scouting a place for our future life as recluses.

Yun had prepared some wine in a flask for us, and the following morning, Honggan turned up at my door just as dawn was breaking. Taking the flask with us, we went out of the city through the Xu Gate and ate our fill at a noodle shop. We then crossed the Xu River and walked to Date Market Bridge in Hengtang, where we hired a small boat.

It was not yet noon when we reached the mountain. Our boatman was a good-natured fellow, so we entrusted him to buy some rice and make lunch, while the two of us went ashore and headed first to Central Peak Temple, south of the Zhixing Sanctuary.

As we followed the path uphill, we saw the temple tucked away in a grove of trees amidst the quiet mountain landscape. The temple being so secluded, the monks had not much to do, but seeing that we were not dressed in formal attire, they did not bid us much welcome. Since our interest was in any case not in the temple, we did not go in. By the time we returned to the boat, lunch was ready to be served.

Meal finished, we set out again, with the boatman coming along with us this time, carrying our wine flask and having instructed his son to watch the boat. From Cold Mountain we hiked on to White Cloud Monastery in the Garden of High Virtue, which had a veranda overlooking a steep cliff. Beneath the veranda there was a small pond surrounded by rockeries and trees, wherein a body of autumn water shimmered. Creeping fig vines draped down the nearby cliff, and the walls of the monastery were all covered with moss. Sitting below the veranda, we could only hear the rustling of falling leaves, the place being bare of human presence.

Outside the gate there was a pavilion. We asked the boatman to sit there and wait, while the two of us entered through a crack in the rock, the so-called Strip of Sky, and followed the steps as they spiraled upwards to the summit, known as Upper White Clouds. There lay the ruins of a convent, of which only a lone shed remained precariously standing. We merely viewed it from afar, rested briefly and then helped each other down.

"You had forgotten to bring your flask on your way up!" the boatman said to us.

"We have come seeking a place for retreat, not just to climb mountains," Honggan explained.

"If you go south from here for two or three *li*, there's a Shangsha Village, with many homes and open land," the boatman said. "I have a cousin by the surname of Fan who lives there. Would you like to go for a visit?"

I was delighted by this and answered, "That's the place Master Xu Qizhai from the late Ming dynasty retreated to. I've heard that the garden there is especially quiet and elegant, but I've never been."

The boatman thus guided us to the village, which was on a road between two hills. The garden was situated on a hillside and had no rockeries within, but there were many old trees with winding branches and lush crowns. Everything from pavilions to window frames, from bamboo fences to thatched cottages, observed the principle of simplicity, making the garden a worthy place for a hermit's retreat. In the courtyard there was also a large acacia tree, two embraces in circumference. Of all the pavilion gardens I have visited, this was the finest.

To the left of the garden was a mountain nicknamed Chicken Coop. The large rocks atop its perpendicular peak bore some resemblance to those seen in Hangzhou's Ancient Cave of Auspicious Stones, but were not as exquisite.

Honggan went to lie down on a blue rock the size of a cot closeby, and remarked, "From here the eye looks up to the peak above and down to the pavilion garden below. The place is as airy as it is secluded—the perfect spot to open our wine flask, I'll say!"

We then bade the boatman to join us for a quaff, singing and howling to our hearts' content.

The village natives, knowing we had come here in search of a certain place, mistakenly thought we had in mind a place with good *feng shui* and told us about such a spot. To this Honggan replied, "We care not for *feng shui* but only for our own liking." Who would have known that this would turn out to be a prophecy?

The wine flask thus emptied, we each went about plucking wild daisies, which we then tucked behind our ears, and returned to the boat just before sundown. When we arrived back at my house at about nine o'clock, the guests were still gathered there.

At this time Yun pulled me aside and said, "Among the actresses there is this Languan[82] who I find dignified in appearance and quite attractive."

I thus called her in on the pretext that my mother wanted to see her. Holding her wrists in my hand, I studied her carefully. She was indeed plump and fair-skinned.

"She is beautiful alright," I turned to Yun and said. "But I feel her appearance does not match up with her name,"

"Well, corpulent people have good fortunes," Yun replied.

"Then where was Yang Yuhuan's good fortune when calamity befell at Mawei?" I retorted.[83]

Yun sent Languan away with an excuse, and then said to me, "Did you get drunk again today?" I then recounted all the sights I had seen that day, and as Yun listened, she became transfixed for quite a while.

---

82. The character Lan bears the meaning of orchid.
83. Here Shen Fu refers to Yang Guifei (c. 719–756), the beloved concubine of Emperor Xuanzong of the Tang dynasty, who is known as one of the Four Beauties of ancient China and who was executed in Mawei during the An Lushan rebellion (755–763).

快

In the spring of Gui Mao,[84] I accompanied Master Sizhai to his position in Weiyang, and that was when I first beheld the visage of Jin and Jiao. Mount Jin is best viewed from afar, while Mount Jiao is best appreciated up close. Unfortunately, in my travels between the two, I never had the chance to ascend them for a view from up high.

Across the Yangtze River to the north, the "green poplars and city walls" in Yuyang's[85] description of Yangzhou came vividly to life. Level Mountain Hall, while just three or four *li* from the city by distance, was eight or nine *li* by road, along which the scenery, though entirely man-made, might rival the mythical emerald pools, phantom gardens or jade palaces with its blend of whimsical design and natural elements. What was remarkable about it was how it laced more than a dozen pavilion gardens together in impressive unity and grandeur, all the way to the mountains.

The foremost quandary in its design must have been the *li*-long stretch of walls between the city and the gardens, for a city view against distant rolling hills is called picturesque, but with a garden slotted in between, it can only be called maladroit. But the arrangement of Level Mountain Hall was so clever—with a pavilion or terrace here and there, allowing glimpses of walls or rockeries, trees or bamboo groves—that no element appeared obtrusive to the visitor at all. Such brilliant handling could only have come from someone with a profound understanding of landscape and composition.

The first garden at the edge of the city was Rainbow Garden, whence a turn north would lead one to a stone bridge called Rainbow Bridge. One wonders if the garden was named after the bridge, or the bridge after the garden. Rowing past the bridge, one would reach the

---

84. 1783.
85. Wang Shizhen (1526–1590), poet of the Ming dynasty.

so-called Long Bank of Spring Willows. The placement of this scene here, and not at the city's edge, further illustrated the craftiness of the design.

Turning further west, one would see a shrine atop a mound called Little Gold Mountain, yet another master stroke, as it rendered the scene delightfully compact with its occlusive effect. I heard that, as a result of the soil in this area being mostly sandy, the builders had made several failed attempts to raise the mound at first before resorting, in the end, to using several planks of wood to hold the earth in place, an endeavor that cost tens of thousands of golds to complete. Who other than the wealthy merchants could have afforded such an undertaking?[86]

Past Little Gold Mountain one saw the Tower of Triumphant Sweep, where every year spectators would congregate to watch dragon boat races. The river below was rather wide, with Lotus Bridge straddling it north to south. The bridge had eight openings and five pavilions in a configuration the Yangzhou locals called "four plates 'round one pot." This design suggested laborious effort but limited imagination and was not the most appealing.

South of the bridge was Lotus Heart Temple, where a white stupa,[87] topped with a golden peak and adorned with tassels, soared into the sky. Pines and cypresses in the courtyard set off the temple's cornices and red walls nicely, while bells and gongs sounded from time to time in the background, a truly unique addition that set this pavilion garden apart from the rest.

Across Lotus Bridge one could see a three-story pavilion with painted beams and upturned eaves dazzling in colors, decorated by Taihu stones and surrounded by white balustrades. This place, called "Where Iridescent Clouds Abound," was to the collection of gardens

---

86. Yangzhou was known for its merchants.
87. A Buddhist shrine with a domed structure at its base, more typical in Western China.

what the centerpiece was to a literary composition. Further ahead was "Morning Sun on Sichuan Ridge," rather unremarkable and with a planeness not living up to the name.

As the mountains loomed closer, the river also narrowed, making four or five bends at places where the waterway was infilled with dirt, with bamboo groves planted atop. And just when it seemed as if the landscape was to exhaust itself, the scene suddenly opened up, revealing the grand vista of Level Mountain's vast pine forest. The words "Level Mountain Hall" were inscribed by none other than Master Ouyang Wenzhong[88] himself.

The so-called "Fifth Best Spring East of Huai" was indeed a mere well inside a man-made grotto, but its water tasted just like spring from the heavens.[89] The other well at the lotus pavilion inside an iron cover bearing six holes was really a sham, its water barely drinkable.

Nine Peaks Garden, located in a quiet area by the South Gate, exuded a distinct, natural charm and was, in my opinion, the finest of all these gardens. As for the Thatched Cottage of Kang Hill, I cannot say how it would compare, having never visited the place myself.

About all these I can of course only provide a rough sketch, an exhaustive description of the finer details and exquisite touches being impracticable. I should add that one must view the gardens as a heavily made-up charmer, rather than comparing them to that renowned natural beauty laundering voile in a brook, in order to really appreciate them.[90]

My visit at the time also coincided with His Majesty's Southern Inspection Tour, for which occasion all renovations had been presently completed. The gardens were presented with great pomp, allowing

---

88. Ouyang Xiu.
89. Rain.
90. Xi Shi, or Shi of the West, one of the Four Beauties of ancient China, who lived circa. fifth century BCE. According to legend, Xi Shi was originally a girl who regularly laundered clothes in the Huansha River.

me to fully enjoy their magnificence in what was truly a once-in-a-lifetime experience.

In the spring of Jia Chen,[91] I accompanied my father to his post at the Wujiang court under a Magistrate He, where I worked alongside several gentlemen including Zhang Pingjiang from Shanyin, Zhang Yingmu from Wulin, and Gu Aiquan from Tiaoxi. There we had the privilege of preparing the provisional palace for the Emperor at Nandouwei, and I thus was able to behold His Majesty's countenance for the second time.

As nightfall approached one day, there arose in me a sudden urge to go back home. At the time, there were these dual-stern dispatch boats with double oars skimming the surface of Taihu Lake, known locally as "water-breaking bridles." I took one and, in a ride so exhilarating that soaring on the back of a crane would not compare, reached the Wu Gate Bridge in the blink of an eye, arriving home before dinner was even ready.

My hometown had always been known for its prosperity, but this particular evening, the displays of extravagance were taken to a far larger scale. The dazzling lanterns were almost blinding to the eye, the music and singing clattering on the ear. Even the "painted beams and carved eaves," "beaded curtains and embroidered drapes," "jade balustrades" and "silk screens" described in ancient literature, could not outshine the scenes from that night.

I was pulled this way and that by my friends to help with floral arrangements and decorations, between which we called on more companions to revel with us in reckless abandon and, being so young with enthusiasm, never tired. Now if I had been born into

---

91. 1784.

this prosperous age but lived in a remote village, how could I have experienced such spectacles?

The same year, Magistrate He was dismissed for some reason, and my father went to work instead for another Magistrate Wang in Haining. From nearby Jiaxing a certain Liu Huijie, a devout Buddhist, came to visit my father.

Liu lived beside Misty Rain Tower in a pavilion overlooking the river named Moon-in-Water Residence, where he would chant sutras and which he kept immaculate as a monk's dwelling. Misty Rain Tower stood in the middle of Mirror Lake, with green poplars lining the surrounding banks but sadly not many bamboo groves. There was also a terrace on the lake affording distant views of fishing boats scattered like stars on the tranquil expanse, which seemed best enjoyed in the moonlight. The vegetarian meals prepared by the monks there were excellent.

In Haining, I worked alongside Shi Xinyue from Baimen and Yu Wuqiao from Shanyin. Xinyue had a son named Zhuheng, who was quiet, composed, and well-mannered, with the refinement of a scholar. He and I got along very well, and he became the second bosom friend I had in this life. Unfortunately, the circumstances of our meeting were such that we did not have much time together, eventually parting like drifting duckweed in the water.

We visited the Chen family's Garden of Sustained Peace, which spanned some hundred *mu*. The place had a multitude of towers, pavilions and winding corridors, as well as a pond quite vast, on which there was a bridge of six bends. The rockeries were covered in vines that hid any chisel mark. Ancient trees stood tall as if they were reaching for the heavens, with birds chirping and flowers falling all around, transporting one to a deep retreat in the mountains. With workmanship that tended to nature, this was the most remarkable among all the rockery gardens I have visited on the flatlands.

We once also held a banquet in the Osmanthus Blossom Pavilion, where the scent of flowers overwhelmed all the flavors and smells of the food, with only the taste of pickled ginger remaining unchanged. Ginger's pungency increases as it ages, and this makes it a fitting metaphor for loyal officials.

Outside the South Gate, the great sea lay immediately before us, with tides coming and going twice daily like long silver embankments breaking through the sea. There were boats that sailed against the tide, and when the tide approached, they would turn around against it, with a long wooden pole resembling a large knife placed at the bow of the boat. As the pole was pressed into the water, the tide would split, opening a passage for the boat to enter. Moments later, the boat would reemerge and, turning back around, ride the receding wave to travel a hundred *li* in no time.

On the embankment, there was a pagoda courtyard, where my father and I watched the tide once on a Mid-Autumn Night. About thirty *li* east of the embankment was Pointed Mountain, with a peak rising abruptly toward the sea. At the summit was a pavilion with a plaque that read "Sea Vast, Sky Boundless," whence one could see, far into the distance, only endless waves crashing into the sky.

When I was twenty-five, I was summoned to Jixi, Huizhou by Magistrate Ke. I boarded a sporting boat[92] from Wulin, passing through Fuchun Mountain, and visited the Fishing Terrace of Ziling. The terrace was halfway up a mountain in the form of a projecting cliff over ten *zhang*[93] above the water. Could it be that in ancient times, the waters had been level with the terrace?

We anchored our boat by a patrol post in Jiekou on a moonlit night. The scene was exactly as described by the lines, "Towering mountains make small the moon; receding water lays bare the stones."

---

92. Likely reference to a kind of floating brothel.
93. One *zhang* is approximately 11 feet.

As for the Yellow Mountain, I regret that I only caught a glimpse of its foot and could not behold its full visage.

Jixi was a small town of simple folk, nestled in the midst of thousands of mountains, including the Stone Mirror Mountain close to town. One would go up the mountain on a path winding for about a *li*, along which waterfalls rushed from precipices above and vegetation shimmered in a dewy emerald.

Halfway up the mountain, there was a stone pavilion surrounded by steep cliffs. The rock on the left side of the pavilion was flat like a screen, blue in color and smooth with sheen enough to reflect one's image. According to legend, the stone once had the power to reveal one's previous incarnation. When Huang Chao passed by, he saw in its reflection the image of a monkey and thereupon set fire to the stone, which put an end to the occult apparitions.

About ten *li* from the area, there was the Cave of Burning Clouds, with jagged rock formations twisting and turning like the landscape of Huanghe Mountain in a most irregular pattern, deep crimson in color.

Nearby, there was a secluded monastery where the salt merchant Cheng Xugu had once invited me for a banquet with meat buns in its midst. A little monk was eyeing the buns greedily and so I handed him four. When I was about to leave, I offered the older monk two barbarian silvers as thanks, which he did not recognize and refused to accept. I thus told him that one barbarian silver could be exchanged for over 700 copper coins, but he still refused on the account that he could not make an exchange nearby. Eventually, I had to gather six hundred copper coins from others, which he accepted gladly.

On a later occasion, I went with the same companions and a wine flask for another visit to the monastery. The older monk told me, "Last time, one of our young monks had an upset stomach from the food, so pray don't offer it again." It was clear that the monks' herbivorous stomachs could not tolerate the richness of meat—truly a pity. I remarked to my companions:

"He who becomes a monk must live in remote places so sequestered from the rest of the world in order to devote himself to the pursuit of truth and peace. Should he live in my hometown on Tiger Hill, where the only sights are flamboyant catamites[94] and courtesans, the only sounds are of strings, pipes and songs, the only smells are of rich delicacies and fine wine, could he still maintain his dried wood of a body, and dead ashes of a heart?"

Another thirty *li* outside the city was a place called Renli, where a flower and fruit fair was held every twelve years, including a potted flower contest in its program. I happened to be in Jixi during such an event and was eager to go but had no sedan chair or horse for transport. I instructed some folks to break bamboo into carrying poles and tie them to a chair to serve as a makeshift sedan. I then hired some carriers for me and my colleague, Xu Ceting, who also came with me, and the sight of us amused a great many along the way.

At the place we arrived at there was a temple, though it was unclear which deity it was dedicated to. In the open area before the temple, a high platform had been set up for theatrical performances, with painted beams and square columns that appeared most lustrous and imposing. However, on closer inspection, these were merely paper cutouts varnished with paint.

At this time gongs were struck and four people carried a pair of candles thick as columns, while another eight carried a swine the size of a buffalo, which had been raised by the community for twelve years before it was now being slaughtered as an offering to the deity.

"This swine sure had a long life, but the god, too, must have sharp teeth," Xu Ceting laughed and said. "Even so, if I were the god, I don't think I would enjoy it."

---

94. Young male sex workers.

"A great display of their artless devotion nonetheless," I replied.

In the corridors and courtyards of the temple, one saw an array of potted plants, Yellow Mountain pines for the most part, which had not been trained but instead selected for their ancient, rugged appearance. In due course the play began, and the crowd surged in like a tide. This was when Ceting and I decided to retreat.

Less than two years later, after some differences with my colleagues, I returned home with a flick of my sleeve. Having witnessed deeds unspeakably sordid in the vanity fair of politics during my time in Jixi, I decided to leave the scholar-official profession behind for commerce.

I had an uncle by marriage, Yuan Wanjiu, who made a living brewing wine by Fairy Pond in Panxi. I invested in his business as a partner along with Shi Xingen. Yuan chiefly sold his wine overseas, and so when the rebellion of Lin Shuangwen in Taiwan blocked the sea routes less than a year later, goods piled up and our investments were lost. I was thus compelled to take up my old profession again. During my subsequent four years of tenure in Jiangbei, there was not a single merry trip worth recording.

Afterwards, while we were at the Free and Easy House, living like earthly immortals, my cousin's husband, Xu Xiufeng, happened to return from eastern Guangdong.

"You cannot plough with your brush and cook morning dew for food in the long run," he exclaimed, seeing that I was idling at home. "Why not travel with me to Lingnan? You ought to be able to make more than a fly's head worth of profits out there."

Yun also encouraged me to go: "While your elders are still in good health and you are still in your prime, why not take this opportunity now to make our pile, instead of constantly pinching pennies like we do?"

With the help of some friends I gathered some funds for this venture. Yun, on the other hand, personally saw to the purchase of embroidery goods, as well as Suzhou wine, drunken crabs, and other items that were not found in Lingnan. After informing my family of the matter, I set out from the Eastern Dam of Wuhu with Xiufeng, on the tenth day of the small spring.[95]

The voyage along the Yangtze River, being my first, filled my heart with great elation and freedom. Every evening as our boat rested at bay, we would have a little drink on the bow. Once, I saw a fisherman using a net no more than three *chi* wide, with holes about four *cun* across and iron hoops at the four corners, which apparently served as sinkers.

"Mencius cautioned us not to exhaust a pond with fine meshes alright," I said in amusement, "but how could such a small, sparse net possibly catch anything?"

"This net is specially designed for catching bream," Xiufeng explained.

I then saw the fisherman tying the net to a long rope, now up, now down, as if to check if there were any fish. After a while, he gave a sudden pull, and a bream indeed came out of water, ensnared in the net.

"I stand corrected. My limited mind simply failed to fathom its cleverness," I sighed.

One day I saw a small, lone peak in the center of the river, and learned from Xiufeng that this was the Little Orphan. Faintly visible in its frosted forest were temples and pavilions of varying heights, but sadly we were whipping downwind and could not stop for a visit.

And when we arrived at the Pavilion of Prince Teng, it dawned on me that Wang Zi'an's description of it in his "Preface" was in fact erroneous, just as he had wrongly placed the Pavilion of Esteemed Scriptures, of my hometown Suzhou's the Prefectural Academy, by

---

95. Tenth month lunar.

the Main Wharf at Xu Gate. From the Pavilion we embarked on a boat with an upturned bow and stern, called *sampan*, and arrived ashore in Nan'an by way of Ganguan. It happened to be my thirtieth birthday that day, and Xiufeng prepared some noodles in my honor.

The following day we passed over Dayu Ridge. At its summit there was a pavilion, with a plaque that read "Overhead the Sun in Reach," referring to its great height. The peak cleft into two steep halves, with a narrow passage in the middle resembling a cobblestone alley, at the opening of which stood two stone tablets, one bearing the inscription, "Bravely recede before the rushing torrent," and the other, "Go no further than the fulfillment of your desire."

At the top of the mountain, there was a shrine to General Mei, of which dynasty I did not know, while the so-called "plum blossoms on the ridge" were nowhere to be found. Perhaps Plum Peak was really named after this General Mei?[96] By this time it was almost the twelfth month, and the potted plum trees I had brought with me were already past their prime, with flowers fallen and leaves turned yellow.

As we crossed over the ridge, the landscape suddenly looked very different. To the west, there was a mountain with delicate stone orifices but whose name I have now forgotten. The boatman told us that there was an immortal's bed inside, but regrettably we did not explore it, having had to pass quickly by.

Upon reaching Nanxiong, we hired an old dragon boat, and as we passed by the township of Foshan, we saw that most of the dwellings there had potted flowers on their roofs, with holly-like leaves, *moutan*-like flowers, and three varieties in bright red, white, and pink. These were camellias.

After finally arriving in the capital of Guangdong on the fifteenth of the twelfth month, we stayed inside Jinghai Gate, renting three

---

96. Mei: Literally, plum.

rooms in a building facing the street from someone by the name of Wang. All Xiufeng's customers were local officials, and following the same list I also made the rounds, which then led to a stream of gift shoppers coming to collect their goods. I sold out everything I had brought within ten days.

On New Year's Eve, the sound of mosquitoes was loud as thunder. The next day, people out celebrating the New Year wore only cotton robes and silk overcoats. Not only was the climate vastly different here, but the local people also had distinct features despite surely sharing the same anatomy.

By the sixteenth day of the first month, three of my fellow townsmen working in court invited me to go to the river to see the doxies,[97] or what the locals call *lau geoi*, in a so-called "tea round."

We set out from Jinghai Gate, taking a small boat shaped like a halved egg and covered by a canopy, and arrived first in Shamian, where so-called flower cruises were all aligned head-to-tail but left a water passage in between for smaller boats to pass through. Each clan had about twenty such boats, connected by horizontal logs to secure them against the sea wind. Between any two boats there was also a wooden stake with a rattan ring around it, which allowed the boats to rise and fall with the tide.

The madams here, referred to as the "coiffured ladies," had their hair wound around a hollow frame of silver wires about four *cun* tall and flowers pinned to their temples with long ear picks. They donned black jackets and slacks that draped over the tops of their feet, had red or green towels tied to their waists, and wore slippers with no socks, like the ones seen on a leading actress in a play.

---

97. Sex workers.

We boarded one of the boats, where the madam bowed to greet us at once, pulling back the curtain for us to enter. Inside, there were some chairs on either side, a large divan in the center, as well as a door leading to astern. As soon as the madam called out that guests were here, we first heard a confusion of footsteps and then saw all the girls come out.

With hair in buns or braids, these girls wore powder thick as wall paint and rouge red as pomegranate flowers. They were dressed in red jackets and green trousers, or vice versa; some wore embroidered butterfly shoes with short stockings, while others were barefoot and wore silver ankle bracelets. Some crouched on the divan, while some leaned by the door, all bright-eyed but not speaking a word.

"What's one to do with all this?" I asked Xiufeng.

"You summon the one you have laid your eyes on," he replied. "Only then will they approach you," he replied.

I tried summoning one, and indeed, she came forward beaming and offered me some betel nuts from up her sleeve. I put one in my mouth and chewed on it but quickly spat it out upon tasting its insufferable bitterness. Wiping my lips with a napkin, I saw that the residue was red as blood. At this the entire company on the boat erupted in laughter.

We next visited the Arsenal to find the girls there similarly dressed and made-up, the only difference being that they could all play the *pipa* regardless of age. When one spoke to them, they would only respond, "*mi*," "*mi*," which meant, "What?"

"They counsel the young to avoid Guangzhou because this place can consume the soul. But whose soul would be seduced by this uncouth makeup and barbarian language?" I remarked.

"Well, the Chao clan girls are styled like fairies. We can try going there," a friend suggested, and thither we went.

The Chao boats were arranged like those at Shamian, and there was a famous madam known as Lady White and dressed like a flower drum singer. Her painted girls all wore high-collared garments with locks around their necks. Their hair touched their eyebrows in front and flowed down to the shoulders in the back, with a maidservant's bun in the center. Those with bound feet wore skirts or dresses, while those with natural feet wore short stockings and butterfly shoes under their draping slacks. While their words were at least intelligible, they still did not rouse any interest, as I found their style a bit too outlandish.

"Across from Jinghai Gate, there is the Yang clan, and they all retain the Wu-style makeup," Xiufeng said. "If you go there, you will surely find someone to your liking."

One of my friends added, "The Yang clan is run by just one madam, known as Widow Shao, accompanied by her daughter-in-law, Big Missie. These two are from Yangzhou, while the rest are indeed from Hubei, Hunan and Jiangxi."

We thus visited the Yang clan. There were only a dozen boats, arranged in two rows across from each other. With hair puffy as clouds and only light makeup, the personas here were all dressed in wide sleeves and long skirts and clear in their speech. The aforementioned Widow Shao greeted us with great enthusiasm. A friend then called for two wine boats, a larger Everlasting Double-Decker and a smaller Sandy Missie Boat, to treat all of us to drinks.

When invited to pick a doxy, I went for a very young one, who vaguely resembled Yun in her figure and visage but also had slim, pointy feet. Her name was Joy. Xiufeng summoned a girl named Missie Emerald, while the rest all had their old acquaintances. Unfastening the boat, we drifted farther from shore and drank with abandon.

As the night wore on, I feared I would not be able to contain myself and insisted on returning home, but the gates to the city had already closed. In coastal cities, the gates close when the sun sets, but this I did not know. Toward the end of the feast, some had laid down to smoke opium, while others were flirting with the doxies on their arms. The servants on the boat brought each person some bedding and pillows in preparation for bedtime.

"Does the main boat also have a place to sleep?" I asked Joy in private.

"There is a garret, but I am not sure if there are guests there tonight," she replied, referring by garret to the attic room of the boat.

"Shall we go see?" I said.

We thus called a small raft to cross over to the Shao boat, whence we could see the other boats forming a long corridor of lights. The madam greeted me, beaming, saying the garret was indeed empty.

"I know we have a distinguished guest here tonight, so I've reserved the garret for you."

"You really are a matchmaking fairy under a lotus leaf!" I smiled and said.

A servant then led us with his candlelight to go upstairs from the ladder in the back, first into a small room furnished with a long chaise on the side as well as a table and chairs, and then behind the curtains to the aforementioned garret. The bed was by the side, above which there was a square glass window. No candle was burning in the room, which was nevertheless bright from the lights on the boats across the river. From the canopied bed to the mirrored vanity, everything exuded opulence.

"The top deck has a nice view of the moon," Joy told me.

We thus opened the window above the ladder and crawled out to reach the top of the stern, enclosed by short railings. A full moon stood before us against the vast water and cloudless sky. Floating on the water like scattered leaves were the wine boats, and twinkling like stars in the sky were their lights. There were also small boats shuttling back and forth. Sounds of *sheng* and string instruments reverberated with the roaring of the long tide, stirring one's emotions.

"This is the real reason one should avoid Guangzhou in his youth!" I said.

At this moment I regretted that I could not have brought my wife, Yun, here to share the view. Looking back at Joy, I saw some vague resemblance under the moonlight. I then put my arms around her to help her descend the terrace, whereafter we put out the candle and lay down together.

Just before dawn, Xiufeng and the others came back to the main boat in great commotion. Hurriedly I put on my robe to go greet them, but they all reproached me for fleeing the previous night.

"I came back here only because I was afraid you might pull back my curtains and lift up my quilt!" I told them. We then went back together to our lodgings.

快

A few days later, I went with Xiufeng to visit Sea Pearl Temple. The temple was on the water and enclosed by walls, as if it was a city. About five *chi* above the water, there was an opening in the wall for a large cannon to defend against pirates. As the tide rose and fell, the cannon also floated up and down, yet the height of the opening did not seem to change. I could not fathom the physics of this phenomenon.

To the west of the Secluded Orchid Gate was the Thirteen Factories, built in an architectural style seen in the Western paintings. On the opposite bank was Blossom Place, which had a profusion of flowers and trees and was where flowers were sold in Guangzhou. Though I had prided myself on knowing most flowers, here I could only recognize about six or seven out of ten. When I inquired about their names, I realized that some were not listed in *The Compendium of Flowers*. Or perhaps this was due to those having different names in the local dialect?

The Sea Pearl Temple was exceedingly vast in scale, with a large banyan tree planted within the mountain gate, more than ten embraces in circumference and with a shade dense like a canopy even in the autumn or winter. The columns, railings, windows, and bars were all made of ironwood. There was also a bodhi tree with leaves resembling those of persimmon trees. When soaked in water and peeled, the flesh of the leaves would become fine and delicate as the wings of a cicada, suitable for binding into little leaflets and transcribing scriptures.

On the way back, we visited Joy at the flower boat. It happened that neither Emerald nor Joy had any guests at the time, so as we made ready to head back after finishing our tea, they insisted on us staying longer. I had wanted to return to the garret, but Big Missie was already entertaining a guest upstairs, so I asked Madam Shao, "Could we all go to my lodging to continue our conversation?" She agreed.

Xiufeng went home first to tell the servants to prepare some wine and fare, with me arriving with Emerald and Joy afterward. As we were enjoying ourselves, Wang Maolao from the county court also turned up, and we invited him to drink with us.

Just as the wine was about to touch my lips, we heard some commotion from below that appeared to be working its way up. It turned out that the landlord's nephew, a local crook, had learned that I was entertaining doxies at home and hired some people to extort me.

"This was all the result of Sanbai indulging in his impulse. I merely followed along," complained Xiufeng.

"Now that we already find ourselves in this situation, we should quickly devise a way to retreat. This is not the time to argue," I said.

Maolao offered, "I will go down and try to talk them out of it."

I then told the servant to hire two sedan chairs immediately, thinking we should help the doxies escape first and then devise a strategy to flee the city together. From upstairs we could hear that Maolao had not been able to dissuade them but had no sign of coming back up either.

The two sedans were now ready outside. I instructed my servant to clear the way ahead. Xiufeng and Emerald followed, and I pulled

Joy along behind, rushing downstairs. Aided by the servant, Xiufeng and Emerald managed to leave the house, but Joy had been grabbed by a man who blocked our way. I gave him a swift kick in the arm, and Joy was able to break free as his grip loosened. Taking advantage of the moment, I also managed to slip away, while my servant remained at the door to ward off anyone coming after us.

"Did you see Joy?" I asked the servant.

"Missie Emerald has left in one of the sedan chairs. I saw Lady Joy come out but did not see her getting into a chair," replied the servant.

I quickly lit a torch and saw that an empty sedan was still by the side of the road. I rushed to Jinghai Gate to find Xiufeng standing by Emerald's sedan.

"She may have gone east but then turned back west," he replied when I made the same inquiry.

I turned around in haste, running past a dozen houses, and suddenly heard a voice calling me in the dark. I then saw under my torchlight that it was Joy. I helped her into the sedan chair and followed along on foot. Xiufeng rushed over to us as well.

"There is a water tunnel by the Secluded Orchid Gate that we can flee from," he said. "I've arranged for someone to bribe the gatekeeper and unlock the gate. Emerald has already gone there. Joy, you must hurry!"

"You go back to the lodge and handle the retreat. I'll take care of Emerald and Joy!" I said.

We reached the tunnel, where the gatekeeper was indeed waiting with the key in hand. Emerald was already inside. With Joy on my left arm, Emerald on the right, we stumbled through the tunnel with arched backs and crane-like footsteps.

It was drizzling outside, and the road was as slippery as grease. We reached Shamian at the peak time of its revelry, where someone on a small boat recognized Emerald and called to us to board. This was when I first saw that Joy's hair was all disheveled, her hairpins and ornaments missing.

"Did they snatch them?" I asked.

She said with a smile, "These were from Mother, and I heard they were all made of solid gold. I had put them away in my purse before going down the stairs, thinking that I would not want to burden you further, for, had they been snatched, you might be asked to compensate."

At this my respect for her only grew. I asked her to put the ornaments back in order and not to tell their Mother what had transpired, but to just say that it was too crowded at our lodging so we decided to return to the boat. Emerald relayed exactly that to the madam, and further told her that we had had some wine and dishes earlier, so some congee would suffice. By this time, the wine guest upstairs had already left.

Madam Shao ordered Emerald to go upstairs with me and Joy as well, and I saw that their embroidered shoes had been soaked with mud. The three of us shared some congee to ease our hunger and chatted by the candlelight. It was then that I learned Emerald was originally from Hunan; Joy, on the other hand, was from Henan, with Ouyang being her surname, and had been sold here by a wicked uncle after her father's passing and mother's remarriage.

Emerald then told me of the hardships in entertaining a constant stream of new guests—having to force a smile when they were unhappy, to drink when they could no more, to keep company when they felt unwell, and to sing when their throats ached.

Worse, there were those unruly guests who would make a scene at the slightest dissatisfaction, hurtling wine cups, flipping the table, and shouting the worst insults and abuse, but their pretend mother, not caring to investigate, would instead criticize them for being remiss. They were also greatly vexed by those wicked guests who would ravage them throughout the night, except Mother still felt some pity for Joy, who was still young and new to the trade.

Having thus spoken, Emerald began to tear up, while Joy also sobbed quietly. I gently pulled Joy into my arms to comfort her. Considering Emerald was Xiufeng's lover, I told her to sleep in the next room.

From then on, every ten days or five, they would send someone to invite me over. Sometimes Joy would take a small boat herself so as to greet me at the riverbank herself. I would always invite Xiufeng every time I went but never any others, nor would I call any other boat. The pleasures of one evening would cost four barbarian silvers at most.

Xiufeng would go from one girl to the other, Emerald today, Carmine tomorrow, in what the locals call "trough hopping," sometimes even taking two doxies at a time. As for me, I kept with Joy, and when occasionally visiting alone, I would either have a small drink with her on the top deck, or talk quietly with her in the garret, without compelling her to sing or drink. I treated her with warmth and care, intending for our boat ride to be as pleasant as possible.

The neighboring doxies all envied her for this. If they were idle and knew I was in the garret, they would always come up for a visit. As such, I got to know all the doxies in the clan, and every time I turned up, I had to respond to greetings left and right, a welcome that could not be bought with wealth.

Over the course of four months, I spent more than a hundred golds at this place but also had the rare pleasure of tasting fresh lychees here. Afterward, the madam insisted that I pay five hundred golds to take Joy as a concubine. Thus badgered, I started planning for my return home. Xiufeng, on the other hand, was reluctant to leave the place. I persuaded him to purchase a concubine, and only then did he agree to return to Wu with me from the same way we had come.

The following year, Xiufeng went back to Guangdong again, but my father would not let me travel with him, so I settled for a position in Magistrate Yang's court in Qingpu. When Xiufeng returned, he spoke of how Joy, seeing that I had not followed along, almost considered ending her life. Alas!

That half year with the Yang clan, like a mere night's dream,
Earned me but the name of heartlessness on the flower fleets.[98]

After my return from Guangdong, I worked in Qingpu for two years, with no noteworthy travels to recount during this time. The meeting between Yun and Han happened not long after, causing a stir in the neighborhood and rendering Yun resentful and more ill. I set up a calligraphy and painting shop with Cheng Mo'an by the door of our house as a means to provide for Yun's medicine and other daily expenses.

Two days after Mid-Autumn, Wu Yunke, along with Mao Yixiang and Wang Wucan, invited me to visit the Little Quiet Room on West Hill. I happened to be busy then so asked them to go ahead furst.

"If you can make it out of the city, meet us at noon tomorrow at the Convent of Crane's Arrival, by the Water Treading Bridge before the mountain," suggested Wu, and I agreed.

The next day, I asked Cheng to stay behind and tend to the shop, while I went out alone through Cheng Gate on foot. I crossed the Water Treading Bridge before the mountain and then walked west along the field ridges until I reached a temple facing south, with a clear stream in front. I knocked to make inquiries.

"What brings you here, sir?" the person inside asked, and I answered. He laughed and said, "This is Cloud Attained. Didn't you see the plaque? Crane's Arrival is already past!"

---

98. A play on the last two lines Du Mu's *Lament* ("Those ten years in Yangzhou, like a mere night's dream, / Earned me but the name of heartlessness in the house of joy.").

"I walked here all the way from the bridge, and did not see any other convent," I said.

"Do you see those thick bamboo growing inside the mud walls?" he pointed in the direction I had come. "That's the one."

I thus walked back to those walls he had referred to, where I saw a small door tightly shut. Peering through the crevice, I saw a winding path flanked by low hedges and lush bamboo groves, with no signs of human presence. I knocked, but there was no answer.

As I stood there, a passerby saw me and advised, "There's a stone in a nook of the wall for knocking on the door." I tried tapping the stone, and indeed, a little monk soon appeared to open the door for me. Following the path, we walked across a small stone bridge and then west before finally reaching the mountain gate. Above the gate hung a black lacquered plaque with the characters "Crane's Arrival" written in white script, as well as a longer epigraph, but I did not stop to read the latter closely.

Once inside the gate, we passed through the Hall of Bodhisattva Weituo[99] to arrive at a room spotlessly clean from top to bottom, from which I inferred that this was none other than the Little Quiet Room.

I then saw a little monk emerge from the left corridor with a teapot, and no sooner had I called out to make inquiries did I hear Xincan's mirthful laughter inside another room, saying, "How's that? Didn't I tell you that Sanbai would never break his word?"

I then turned around to see Yunke come out to greet me. He said, "We've been waiting for you for breakfast, why were you so late?"

A monk followed behind and bowed to me, introducing himself as Monk Zhuyi. I then went into the room to see it was quite small, spanning only three beams and with a plaque that read *Osmanthus Pavilion*, which referred to the two osmanthus trees in the courtyard

---

99. Bodhisattva Skanda, devoted guardian of Buddhist monasteries who protects the teachings of Buddhism.

in full bloom at the time. Seeing me enter, Xingcan and Yixiang both heckled, "Penalty of three cups to the latecomer!" On the table a fine mix of both vegetarian and meat dishes had been laid out, paired with both yellow wine and white liquor.

"How many places have you visited so far?" I asked.

"We arrived last night, and only managed to visit Cloud Attained and the River Pavilion this morning," Yunke replied.

I joined them in drinking, one round after another. After the meal, we toured, including again Cloud Attained and the River Pavilion, eight or nine places together, and went as far as Hua Mountain. Each place had its own appeal, and I cannot begin to describe them all.

At the top of Hua Mountain there was a Lotus Flower Peak, but as it was already getting dark, we agreed to visit another time together and did not go further. It was here that the osmanthus blossoms reached their utmost profusion, and we each savored a cup of green tea under the flowers before taking the mountain sedan chairs back to Crane's Arrival.

To the east of Osmanthus Pavilion, there was another small pavilion called Vicinity of Cleanliness, where the table had been already set. Zhuyi sat with us, seldom saying a word, but was nevertheless a hospitable host and a good drinker. At first we plucked osmanthus twigs as wagers for our drinking game, and later we simply went around drinking, which did not cease until the second watch of the night.[100]

"The moon is quite beautiful this evening. Falling into a drunken stupor like this would be a squandering of this clear light," I said. "Shall we find some place high and airy to enjoy the moonlight, so that we may not waste this gentle night?"

"The Pavilion of Crane's Release is a good place," suggested Zhuyi.

"Xingcan has brought his lute along," said Yunke, "but we have not heard the virtuoso play yet. How about we hear it there?"

---

100. Between 9 p.m. and 11 p.m.

We thus all went along, bringing the lute with us, and on the way only smelled the sweetness of osmanthus and saw long stretches of frosted forest. The sky was immense beneath the moon, and everything had fallen silent. Xingcan played *Three Variations on the Plum Blossom*, whence we were transported to a realm not of this earth. Inspired, Yixiang also took out the iron flute from up his sleeve and piped softly along.

"Among those viewing the moon at Stone Lake tonight, who could find pleasure close to ours?" Yunke said.

By this he was referring to the moon-viewing festivities in our Suzhou, which took place on eighteenth of the eighth month every year under the Bridge of Cruising Spring on Stone Lake, where swarming tour boats would fill the whole evening with music and revelry. A moon-viewing event in name only, it was actually just an occasion for some drunken affairs with the doxies.

Soon the moon fell and frost froze, and we returned to the garden and retired to bed.

The next morning, Yunke asked the group, "There is a Convent of Candor nearby, very much secluded. Have any of you been there?"

All of us replied that, not only had we been, we had not so much as heard of the place.

"Candor is closed off by mountains in all directions. It's a very remote place, and even the monks can't stay there for long," Zhuyi said. "I visited it once last year, and it had already collapsed. Afterward, it was rebuilt by the lay devotee Peng, but I haven't been back since. However, I can still vaguely recognize the place. If you wish to visit, it would be my honor to guide you."

"We are not going on an empty stomach, are we?" Yixiang asked.

Zhuyi laughed and said, "We have already prepared some noodles. I'll also have the Taoist priest bring a wine flask to accompany us."

Having had our fill thus, we set off on foot. As we passed by the

Garden of High Virtue, Yunke said he wanted to visit the White Cloud Monastery there, so we all went in and sat down. A monk came out in a slow gait, folded his hands to greet Yunke, and said, "It's been two months since I last saw you. What news is there in the city? Is the Governor still in his place?"

At this moment Yixiang abruptly stood up, said, "Baldface!" and then walked out with a flick of the sleeve. Holding back our laughter, Xingcan and I followed him. Yunke and Zhuyi exchanged mere pleasantries with their interlocutor before also excusing themselves.

The Garden of High Virtue was where the Honorable Fan Wencheng was buried, and the White Cloud Monastery was right by it. A veranda in the monastery faced a steep precipice overhung with vines of creeping fig. Below it there was a pond a *zhang* wide, with golden koi swimming around in its clear, turquoise water, aptly named Monk's Bowl Spring. There was also a small tea stove in a secluded corner. The view from the lush green groves behind the pavilions included an overlook of the layout of Fan Garden. It was a pity that the monk was so vulgar, making us loath to stay any longer.

From there we passed Upper Sand Village and hiked Chicken Coop Mountain, reaching the same summit that Honggan and I had once mounted. Seeing that the scenery remained the same but Honggan was no more, I could not help lamenting the cruelty of life's vicissitudes.

While I was walking along, lost in my wistful meditation, we suddenly came upon a rushing torrent, which blocked the path ahead. A few village children foraging for mushrooms in the weeds nearby peeked out and giggled, seemingly surprised by the presence of our large group. I asked for the way to Candor and was told, "The water ahead is too rapid to cross. Return to Shuwu, take the southern path there to go over the ridge, and you will get there."

We followed their directions and walked for another *li* after crossing the ridge before noticing the surrounding groves were becoming denser and denser. The path itself was also overgrown with moss and devoid of human traces.

"It seems we are close, but the path is hard to make out," said Zhuyi as he surveyed our surroundings. "What should we do?"

I squatted down and carefully observed the area. Among thousands of bamboo stalks, I saw the faint outline of a jumble of rocks and some walls. We crossed over, brushing aside the bamboo in our way, to find a small gate with a plaque that read, "The Chan Convent of Candor, restored by Peng, 'Old Man of South Garden,' on date such-and-such."

My friends were all pleased, exclaiming, "Had it not been for you, this place would be impossible to find much like Peach Blossom Spring!"

The mountain gate was tightly shut, and we knocked for a long time but received no response. Suddenly, a side door creaked open, and a young man dressed in shabby garb came out. His face was pale, and his shoes were worn out.

"What brings you here?" he asked.

Zhuyi bowed and said, "We have long heard of the peacefulness of this place and have come specially to pay a visit."

"This is a destitute temple with very few monks to begin with. I'm afraid we won't be able to attend to you. Pray look elsewhere for your tour."

With that, he turned to close the door, but Yunke hurriedly stopped him, promising that if he would let us in, we would certainly pay him for the trouble.

The young man smiled and said, "We haven't even any tea to offer and could only hope you don't mistake our privation for slight. How could we expect any reward?"

He then opened the door. Inside, we saw the face of Buddha radiating golden rays of light against the green umbras of the trees. The stone bases of the courtyard columns were embroidered with moss.

Behind the temple, the steps were almost perpendicular as a wall, with balustrades on both sides. Following these steps to the west, we came across a rock in the shape of a steam bun and about two *zhang* high, with fine bamboo palms encircling its base.

Turning further north, we ascended a slanted corridor to reach a guest hall spanning three beams and facing a big rock. Below the rock there was a small moon-shaped pond, with clear spring water flowing through and water weeds crisscrossing therein. The main temple lay east of the guest wall, with the monks' bedchambers and the kitchen on its left, and a steep cliff rising behind it. The trees here were so dense that they obscured the sky.

An exhausted Xingcan sat down by the pond for a rest, and I followed suit. Just as I was about to open the wine flask for a small drink, I suddenly heard Yixiang's voice coming from the treetops above, calling out, "Sanbai, come quick! Here is a marvelous view!"

I looked up but Yixiang was not in sight. Xingcan and I followed his voice to come out through the east wing, whence we turned north. After mounting several dozens of stone steps steep like a ladder, we glimpsed a tower among the bamboo groves and proceeded to ascend it.

The top of the tower had a plaque that read *Flying Cloud Pavilion* as well as eight gaping windows. Nearby mountains surrounded us like city walls, with only an opening in the southwest corner, through which one could see in the distance a body of water touching the sky and some faint silhouettes of sails on its surface. This was none other than Taihu Lake. Leaning against the windows, one looked down to see bamboo leaves swaying in the rustling wind, like waves of wheat.

"So what do you say?" asked Yixiang.

"This is truly a marvelous view," I replied.

Just at that moment we heard Yunke call out from west of the tower, "Yixiang, come quick! Here the view is still more marvelous!"

We thus descended the tower and, after mounting another dozen steps to its west, reached an open deck as broad as a stage. We reckoned that this place was now above the steep cliff behind the temple and, judging from the remaining ruins, believed this to be the site of the old temple.

The deck afforded an even more expansive view of the mountains than that at the top of the tower. Yixiang howled in Taihu Lake's direction, and the mountains all echoed in response.

We sat down on the ground and opened our wine casket, but realized we were hungry. The young man offered to cook some dry rice for us to make up for the temple's want of tea, but at our suggestion agreed to make some congee instead.

We invited him to eat with us, and asked him how the place had fallen into such a plight, to which he answered, "We have no neighbors here, and back when our pantry was filled, the food was all taken by the night burglars. Even the vegetables and fruits we planted ended up enriching the woodcutters.

"This a branch of Chongning Temple, which entitles the kitchen to receive a monthly ration of one stone[101] of dry rice and one jar of pickled vegetables," he continued. "I'm a descendant of Peng and only staying as a temporary caretaker of the place. When I leave, which will be soon, this place will likely be completely deserted."

Yunke thanked him with a barbarian silver. When we returned to Crane's Arrival, we hired a boat to head back to the city. Later I made a painting depicting Candor, both as a gift to Zhuyi and as a record of this merry trip.

That same winter, due to some trouble arising out of my guarantee of a friend's debt, I lost my family's favor and had to move out to the

---

101. About 30 kilograms, or 66 pounds.

Hua family's residence in Xishan. The following spring, I wished to go look for employment in Yangzhou but was short on funds. An old friend, Han Chunquan, was employed at the Shanghai court then, and I decided to pay him a visit.

I felt it inappropriate to enter the court in my ragged clothes and worn-out shoes, and so in my letter I had asked to meet instead in the County Temple Garden Pavilion. Upon seeing me, Chunquan sympathized with my plight greatly and aided me with ten golds.

The garden we met in had been built on donations from maritime merchants and was certainly very grand—a pity, however, that its landscape was rather jumbled and devoid of any organizing principle, as evidenced by the rockeries lying at the back of the garden in complete lack of consonance with each other. On my way back, I suddenly recalled the beauty of Yushan and was by chance able to hitch a boat thereto.

It was the middle of spring, the time when peach and plum blossoms vied for beauty, yet I was traveling all this way without a companion. With my three hundred bronzes I meandered, eventually arriving at the Yushan Academy. From outside the wall, I looked up to see trees and flowers in exquisite clusters of green and red. The academy itself was nestled between mountain and water, which lent it a peaceful charm. Unable to find the gate, I had to ask for directions.

On my way there, I came across a tea stand and decided to stop for a rest. The Biluochun tea was most excellent. I asked around for the best places to visit in Yushan, and a traveler replied, "Go out the West Gate from here, and you will arrive at the Sword Gate, which has the best view in Yushan. If you wish to go, I should be happy to guide you there." I gladly agreed.

We went out from the West Gate and walked along the foot of the mountain for several *li* before seeing its peak gradually emerge tall before us, with horizontal lines on its rock surface. When we approached closer still, we saw the peak cleave into two jagged halves, towering over several dozen *ren*.[102] Viewed up close from below, the cliffs looked as if they were about to tip over.

"It is said that there is a cave dwelling above with otherworldly views," said the traveler. "A pity, though, that no path leads there."

Already roused by his words, I rolled up my sleeves and proceeded to scale the cliff like a monkey, heading straight for the summit. The so-called cave dwelling was only about a *zhang* deep, with an opening allowing a view of the sky above. But the view down made my knees so weak that I almost stumbled and fell. On my descent, I had to cleave my belly to the cliff and clutch onto the vines tightly for safety.

"Truly impressive!" the man exclaimed. "Your carefree travel spirit is unmatched by anyone I've seen."

Now parched and in want of a drink, I invited the man to join me at a roadside tavern, where we each had three cups of wine. I had not yet fully explored the area when the sun began to set. I picked up some dozen red stones and carried them back to my inn. That night, I boarded a boat to Suzhou, and subsequently arrived back in Xishan. Such was my merry trip in the midst of sorrow and distress.

In the spring of Jia Zi, during the reign of Emperor Jiaqing,[103] having just been stricken by my father's death, I almost left home to live far away as a recluse and only stayed at the urging of my dear friend, Xia Yishan, who kindly offered to accommodate me in his own home. That autumn, in the eighth month, Yishan invited me to accompany him on a trip to the East Sea to collect farm rents on Yongtai Sands, which was in the jurisdiction of Chongming Island.

We set sail from Liu River Mouth, traveling over a hundred *li* by sea before reaching the Sands, a virgin land that had just been formed

---

102. One ren is approximately five feet.
103. 1804.

from new sediments.[104] There were no markets or streets here. A vast expanse of reeds and bulrushes lay before us, giving away few signs of human habitation, save for a handful of warehouses encircled by a moat, with willows on its banks. These belonged to Yishan's fellow tradesman Ding.

Known by his courtesy name Shichu, Ding was a Chongming native who had established himself as the leading settler on the Sands. His accountant was a man named Wang. They were both jolly fellows, fond of guests and unburdened by formalities, and upon first meeting me they were already treating me like an old friend, going as far as slaughtering a swine and emptying their wine jugs for our entertainment.

When they drank, they only knew to play the finger-guessing game, being strangers to poetry and literature; when they sang, they only knew to howl, being equally uninitiated in music; and finally when they were drunk, they had the workers spar and wrestle for our amusement.

On the estate there were over a hundred buffalos, which would simply stay unsheltered at night on the banks. There were also some geese that were kept to alert against pirates. By day, Shichu would go hunting with hawks and dogs among the reeds and sandbars, the game consisting mostly of birds. I, too, joined in these pursuits, and would doze off anywhere when weary.

Once Shichu took me to a ripe field, where each farm was numbered, with tall dikes raised around it to protect against the tide. These dikes were equipped with sluices for water regulation, which would open during the dry season to irrigate, and close during the rains to drain away the excess.

The farm hands, scattered like stars across the fields, would come running at a single cry, addressing Shichu as their Land Master in the

---

104. Slow accumulation of sediment from the Yangtze River.

most respectful and obedient manner. They were endearingly simple and sincere. If provoked unjustly, they could be as surly as wolves and tigers, but they were just as easily pacified by words that appealed to their sense of fairness.

The weather here was capricious, evocative of primeval times. I could often see from my bed waves crash violently, and hear from my pillow tides beating like drums. One night, I suddenly caught sight of a red lantern the size of a basket floating several dozen *li* away on the sea, the sky above it also illuminated by the glow, as if on fire.

"This divine light and divine fire here," explained Shichu, "are an omen that the sands will soon rise up again to form new land."

At this Yishan, ever the free spirit, grew more wanton, and I, too, let go of all inhibitions, singing on the back of a buffalo one moment and dancing drunk upon the sands the next, all according to my fancy. This merry trip was when I felt the most liberated in my life.

Business done, Yishan and I returned in the tenth month.

Among the sights of Tiger Hill in my Suzhou, my favorite is Thousand-Acre Cloud at the back of the hill, followed by the Sword Pond. The rest are largely works of human artifice, tainted by a kind of affected vanity and having lost their natural beauty.

The newly constructed Bai Memorial Hall and Tower Shadow Bridge are graceful only in name. The Shore of Iron Forge brings to mind a woman in gaudy makeup. I thus refer to it in jest as the Shore of Rural Flores.[105]

Even the famous Lion Grove, being the brainchild of Master Yunlin and for all its exquisite rocks and ancient trees, seems on the whole little more than a heap of coal dust bedecked with moss and

---

105. The originals of Shore of Iron Forge and Shore of Rural Flores are near-homophones.

ant holes, without any evocation of elevated hills or vast forests. My uncultivated eye fails to see its merit.

The Mountain of Mystic Rock, once the site of the Palace of Reigning Beauty erected by the King of Wu, houses such famous spots as Xi Shi Cave, Corridor of Echoing Steps, and the Fragrance-Plucking Path. But its sprawling landscape feels scattered and in want of tightening, and I find it far inferior to secluded Tianping or Zhixing, each of which has a distinct beauty.

Mount Dengwei, otherwise known as Yuan Tomb, faces Taihu Lake to its west and Peak Brocade to its east. Its terra cotta cliffs and green pavilions are out of a painting. The mountain dwellers here make a living raising plums, and when in bloom, blossoms white as snow will cover an area of dozens of *li*, hence the name, Sea of Fragrant Snow.

To the left of the mountain there are four ancient cypress trees known by the names of Pure, Rare, Ancient, and Strange. Pure has a lean trunk that stands tall and upright and a luxuriant crown evocative of a green umbrella. Rare squats low to the ground with three bends in its trunk, resembling the character "之". Ancient is bald on top and stout in build, with one half withered, revealing beneath the form of a human palm. Strange has a trunk and branches that coil like the shell of a snail. It is said that these trees date far back to the Han dynasty.

In the early spring of Yi Chou, I was invited by Yishan's venerable father, Chunxiang, to join him and his younger brother, Jieshi, as well as his four sons and nephews, on a trip to their ancestral temple at Mount Fu for that year's spring sacrifices and tomb sweeping.

On our way we stopped by at the Mountain of Mystic Rock and, via the Tiger Mountain Bridge and Feijiahe, arrived at the Sea of Fragrant Snow to view the blossoms, within which the ancestral temple was nestled. The plum blossoms were in peak bloom then, with a fragrance that perfumed even the human breath. Subsequent to this trip, I painted a twelve-volume work titled *The Mount Fu Kingdom of Wind and Wood* for Jieshi.

In the ninth month of that same year, I accompanied my friend Shi Zhuotang along on a voyage up the Yangtze River for a position he had been newly appointed to in Chongqing, Sichuan.

We first arrived at Wancheng. At the foot of Mount Wan[106] lay the tomb of the Honorable Yu, a loyal official of the Yuan dynasty. To the side of the tomb there was a three-beamed hall by the name of Grand View Pavilion, with South Lake in its front and Lurking Mountain in its back.

The pavilion was placed on the ridge of the mountain, proffering a clear and open view into the distant landscape. To its side there was a long corridor with windows open to the north, through which one could see foliage dressed in peak crimson, bright as spring blossoms. My companions on this trip were Jiang Shoupeng and Cai Ziqin.

Just outside the South Gate there was Wang's Garden, which stretched long from east to west, and shorter along the other orientation, as it was bordered by the city to its north and the lake to its south. Such constraints must have made it difficult to devise an appropriate layout, but it appeared that a solution was found in the method of using stacked terraces and storied pavilions.

By stacked terraces I mean that courtyards were raised above rooftops and bedecked with rockeries or plants, making the visitor forget that there were indeed houses beneath their feet. With a rockery courtyard, the structure below could be solid, whereas with a garden the structure beneath would have to be hollow, so as to allow the plants to still live off the energy of the earth.

By storied pavilions I mean that atop of the house there would be an open gallery, further atop which there would be a courtyard. The

---

106. Now known as Tianzhu Mountain.

entire structure interlocked four levels together, complete with a small pond that somehow managed without leakage, wherein it was difficult to discern between solid and hollow. All the bases were entirely made of brick and stone, with pillars constructed in the Western style. Being right across the South Lake, the garden was also blessed with an unobstructed view. Freely roaming within, I felt it superior to many of the plane gardens. It was truly a marvel of human ingenuity.

The Yellow Crane Tower[107] of Wuchang stands atop Yellow Swan Rock, with Yellow Swan Mountain behind it, commonly known as Snake Mountain. Its three stories, all with painted beams and upturned eaves, tower over the city and face the Qingchuan Pavilion across from Yangtze River in Hanyang.

Zhuotang and I braced the snow one day to ascend it, whence we beheld gem-like snowflakes swirling in the vast sky toward silver mountains and jade trees in the distance, as if we were already in the immortal land. Small boats crisscrossed on the river below, drifting like fallen leaves amidst the waves. This was a view that could chill any ambition and desire. The walls here were covered with numerous inscriptions and odes, most of which I cannot recall now, except for this one couplet:

When the yellow crane returns
  let us pour from our gold cups
    over the millenia-old meadows on these banks and isles
Even the white clouds depart
  who then will play the jade flute
    toward the fifth-moon plum blossoms in the riverside city

---

107. The Yellow Crane Tower: A landmark of literary significance, having inspired a plethora of Chinese poems over different dynasties, the foremost of which may be "The Yellow Crane Tower" by Cui Hao (704–754).

The Red Cliffs[108] of Huangzhou rise high outside the Hanchuan Gate of the city over a riverbank, perpendicular as a wall. Its rocks are all of a crimson hue, hence the name. In the *Water Classic*, it is referred to as the Red Nose Mountain. Dongpo, upon his visits, composed two odes, saying this was the place where the Wu and Wei armies battled, but that is not the case. Beneath the cliffs, what used to be a river has long dried up since, and now there is a Pavilion of Two Odes on the new land.

In the middle of winter that year, we arrived in Jingzhou. Zhuotang had received an official letter appointing him to oversee Tongguan and asked me to stay in Jingzhou. For that regrettable reason I did not get the opportunity to see the mountains and waters of Sichuan.

When Zhuotang reached Sichuan, his son Dunfu and the rest of the family, along with Cai Ziqin and Xi Zhitang, also remained in Jingzhou, and we all resided in the abandoned garden of the Liu family.

I recall that the hall had a plaque that read "The Wisteria and Red Trees Mountain House," and that the courtyard, enclosed by stone balustrades, had in it a square pond measuring about one *mu*. In the center of the pond there was a pavilion, which was accessible by a stone bridge and behind which some soil and rockeries had been laid, now overgrown with vegetation. The rest of the garden was largely empty, save for some dilapidated buildings and pavilions.

With few worries during this sojourn in Jingzhou, we spent our time singing or reciting poems, going out on excursions or gathering together to chat. Though we were bare of cash as the year drew to a close, all of us were in good spirits. We pawned our clothes to buy wine as well as some gongs and drums to celebrate the New Year, and so there would be libations every evening without fail, as well as drinking games to go with them. In the worst of times, we would make do with

---

108. Similarly of great literary significance on account of Su Shi's odes.

a little cheap liquor, but still we always made sure that the toasts were carried out with great ceremony.

Once, I met a fellow townsman by the surname of Cai, who turned out, after he and Cai Ziqin talked over their genealogy, to be related to the latter, and who kindly offered to show me the famous sights of the region.

We visited the Tower of Winding River in front of the Prefectural Academy, the place Zhang Jiuling, during his time as secretary general here, used to write his poems. There is also Zhu Zi's poem thereof that goes:

> *In my wistful longing I wish to return thither,*
> *but in its place ascend the Tower of Winding River.*

Above the city there was also the Tower of Mighty Chu, which was built by the Gao family during the Five Dynasties and, with its grand scale and towering height, afforded a view hundreds of *li* into the far distance. From here one saw the city encircled by water, with weeping willows on its banks and small boats rowing back and forth, a picturesque scene.

The Jingzhou court, once the headquarters of General Guan Zhuangmiao, had inside its gate a broken stone trough, which was said to be the trough where the legendary Red Hare once fed. I tried to visit the residence Luo Han, supposed to be on a small lake in the western part of the city, but could not find it. I then visited the former residence of Song Yu in the northern part of the city. During the Hou Jing Rebellion, when Yu Xing fled the capital and returned to Jiangling, it was in Song Yu's old residence that he stayed. The place had since been turned into a tavern, no longer recognizable.

It was frigid on the last day of the year in snowfall's wake. With the New Year thus ushered in, we were spared the usual obligations of paying courtesy calls and instead spent the day lighting firecrackers, flying kites, and making paper lanterns for amusement.

By and by, with flowers blooming at the cue of spring wind and spring dust now washed away by the rain, Zhuotang's concubines came down from the river along with his little daughters and sons. Dunfu thus began to pack, and we all left together for a voyage up the river, whence we went onshore in Fancheng and then headed straight to Tongguan.

We traveled westward from Wenxiang County in Henan through Hangu Pass to see an inscription which read "Purple *Qi* Comes from the East," marking the place Laozi once passed through on the back of a black buffalo. The path between the two mountains was narrow, barely allowing two horses to walk side by side.

About ten *li* from there lay Tongguan, which was flanked by steep cliffs on its left and the Yellow River on its right. A fortress was erected at this strategic location with the most imposing towers and formidable ramparts, yet there was hardly any traffic and few living souls around. There is the Changli verse that goes, "The sun shines on Tongguan, its four gates open wide." Perhaps he, too, was referring to the desolation of the place?

Under the Inspectorate there was only a lieutenant inspector. The official residence abutted the northern wall of the city, with a garden in its back roughly three *mu* from left to right. The west side and east side of the garden each had a pond, with water channeled in from the southwestern wall and running eastward to a point between the two ponds, whence it split into three channels: one flowed south toward the main kitchen for daily use, another flowed east into the eastern pond, and the third turned north, then west, spouting into the western pond through the stone dragon mouth. From there, the water further turned northwest and, through a sluice, flowed northward and was finally released through a hole at the foot of the city wall into the Yellow River.

The steady burble of water running day and night was refreshing to the ear, and amidst the dense bamboo groves in the garden one could barely see the sky above. In the center of the western pond there was a pavilion with lotus flowers on both sides.

East of the pond there was a south-facing studio with three rooms, as well as a courtyard with a trellis covered in grapevines, beneath which a square stone table could be used for chess games or drinking. The rest of the courtyard consisted solely of chrysanthemum beds.

West of the pond there was an east-facing veranda with three rooms, whence one could sit and listen to the sound of flowing water, or enter the inner chambers through a small door on the south end. Beneath the windows on the northside lay yet another small pond, with a small shrine to its north, dedicated to the flower goddesses.

In the center of the garden, a three-story tower stood level in height with the northern city wall. From the top, one could look out upon the Yellow River right outside the city. The mountain ranges north of the river formed a screen in what was already within the territory of Shanxi, a most magnificent sight.

For my part, I resided in the southern part of the garden in a studio in the shape of a boat. The courtyard had within it a mound with a small pavilion on top, which afforded a view of the entire garden, as well as trees on all sides, whose umbras provided shelter from the summer heat. Zhuotang referred to my studio as "The Boat Untethered," and it was the best lodging I had stayed in since the beginning of my travels.

On the mound there were also dozens of varieties of chrysanthemums, though before they bloomed we had taken residence up elsewhere at the Tong Mountain Academy, as Zhuotang had been appointed to another post as Provincial Judge in Shanzuo.

With Zhuotang gone, Ziqin, Zhitang and I were left with not much to attend to and so went on frequent excursions. Once we went on horseback to the Huayin Temple, passing through Huafeng, where during the time of Yao locals used to offer the three prayers to the emperor.[109]

Inside the temple there were many ancient locust trees and cypresses, all three or four embraces in circumference. There were also locust trees growing from inside the cypress trees, and vice versa. The temple hall boasted an abundance of ancient tablets, including inscriptions of "Fortune" and "Longevity" by Chen Xiyi.

At the foot of Mount Hua was the Courtyard of Jade Spring, the place where Master Xiyi departed his earthly body. There was a cave here the size of a small room, with a statue of Master Xiyi reclining on a stone bed. The water here was clear, the sand bright, the grass mostly crimson, the spring water rapid and surrounded by bamboo.

Outside the cave, there was a pavilion with a plaque that read "The Worry-Free Pavilion." Beside it stood three ancient trees, with barks resembling cracked charcoal and leaves like those of the locust tree, though darker in color. I did not know their proper name but the locals simply called these "worry-free trees." The majestic Mount Hua towered who-knows-how-many thousand *ren*, and it was a pity that we did not have enough provisions to last through a trip there.

On our way back, we came upon a grove of persimmons readily ripe and golden. From atop my horseback I picked one and started eating it right then and there, despite the locals' calls of warning. As I bit into the persimmon, an astringent taste spread in my mouth. Quickly spitting it out, I dismounted my horseback and searched for a spring to rinse my mouth, and only then was I able to speak again. The locals all laughed heartily and explained that one must boil persimmons first to rid them of their astringency. Of this I was of course ignorant.

---

109. According to *The Zhuangzi,* the legendary Emperor Yao was offered three prayers when visiting Hua — longevity, fortune, and many sons — which Yao declined, on account that none of the three were of use in nourishing virtue.

In the beginning of the tenth month, Zhuotang sent a messenger from Shandong to retrieve his family, and we all left Tongguan for Shandong, passing Henan. In the western part of Shandong's capital, Ji'nan, there was the famous Lake Brilliance, home to many such famous scenic spots as Lixia Pavilion and the Pavilion of Water Fragrance. I heard it was a delightfully serene experience to boat here and drink wine under the dense willow shades, where the air would be infused with the scent of lotus flowers. But it was winter at the time of my visit, and I saw only withered willows and cold mists on a vast expanse of water—nothing more.

The Baotu Spring is the greatest of the seventy-two springs in Ji'nan, and consists of three holes, each gushing as if boiling water were bubbling up from below ground. Most springs flow from above, but this one rises from below, which is quite the oddity. Above the spring there is a pavilion, which houses a statue of Lü the Progenitor and where many visitors like to gather for tea tasting.

In the second month of the following year, I relocated again for an official position in Laiyang. Then in the autumn of Ding Mao, when Zhuotang was demoted to serve instead in the Hanlin Imperial Academy, I followed him along to the capital. As for the oft-talked about ocean mirages of Dengzhou,[110] I never had the chance to see them.

---

110. Ocean mirages in Dengzhou: This phenomenon in Dengzhou (now Penglai District, Yantai, Shandong Province) was the subject of Su Shi's poem, "Ocean Mirage at Dengzhou."

AFTERWORD

In the early 20th century, the fictious author Pierre Menard wrote Don Quixote. The text coincided "word for word and line for line," with the classic satire of Spanish chivalry, written by Miguel De Cervantes. But stripped of its 17th century context, Don Quixote transforms into a different text. The 20th century novel Don Quixote – as described to us by Jorge Louis Borges, the author of the short story Pierre Menard, Author of the Quixote – contains brazenly pragmatic ideas and transcends its predecessor. In other words, to the story's narrator, Don Quixote is a better book in the 20th century than in the 17th: "The Cervantes text and the Menard text are verbally identical, but the second is almost infinitely richer."

All books have three contexts: that of the author when written, of the book when published or rediscovered, and the reader when read. Transport a book to a different time and its context can transform it.

Roughly a century before Menard, the writer Shen Fu composed Six Records of a Floating Life. About 70 years later, a man named Yang Yin stumbled upon the manuscript and gave it to his brother, who published the extant four of the six records to great acclaim.

Think of how the context has evolved since Yang found the text in an old book shop – one imagines the pages dusty but bright, splayed open like the entry into a great dream.

Shen was born near the Pavilion of Azure Waves in 1763, under the reign of Emperor Qianlong in the "heyday of peace and prosperity," before the decades of wars, wars, wars – the most devastating of which, the apocalyptic Taiping Rebellion, caused the deaths of tens of millions of people. Yang found the book in the decade following the 1860s extermination of the Taiping Rebellion, with Shen's musings pleasantly clashing with the discord of the time.

In the 1930s – when China was a failed state, trampled over by warlords, the Nationalists, the Communists, and the Japanese – the Chinese modernist Lin Yutang published his first translation of the book. He applauded the female protagonist as one of the "loveliest women in Chinese literature," and described the book as the "simple story of two guileless creatures in search of beauty." Guileless and contemporaneously unequal: Shen relishes the gift of "a concubine, ushering me back into the spring dream of life." After Mao Zedong conquers China in 1949, he ends the practice of foot-binding and concubinage.

Six Records did not reflect the Maoist reality of life, and Mao-era Communists denigrated the book for its "petit bourgeois ambience" and for encouraging "separating oneself from the life of workers, formers, and soldiers."

Mao died in 1976. In 1981, after reading the book, the playwright Yang Jiang decided to write her experiences of being sent down during the Cultural Revolution,[111] the anarchic 1966-1976 period where Mao whipped the entire nation into paranoia and hysteria. Her "Six Records of a Cadre School" helped spark a trend of literary works processing one of China's great historical traumas, through the "trifles" of existence.

I first read this book as a student at Columbia University, where I graduated with a degree in East Asian Languages and Cultures in 2006. I saw myself as bold, impulsive, taking great gulps of this new world. In his 1982 book China: Alive in the Bitter Sea, the journalist Fox Butterfield recalls asking a Harvard librarian for Chinese language tapes in the 1950s. She "peered at me over the top of her glasses as if I had stumbled into the wrong church," he wrote. 'Chinese? Chinese?' she repeated. 'Isn't Chinese a dead language?'" The field had

---

111. https://paper.people.com.cn/hqrw/html/2016-06/06/content_1725928.htm

exploded over that half-century. But when I studied it at Columbia, Chinese still felt like a secluded garden of a language, guarded by pictographs.[112] Learning Chinese and studying Chinese literature was delightful and unmooring, and Six Records had an ethereality, a compelling flightiness: I remember envying the drinking parties and the decadence, where the girls are "plump and fair-skinned" and where "tender green and delicate cerise vied for beauty."

I read Alex Fang's delightful new translation in May 2025, on the day that Secretary of State Marco Rubio restricts Chinese students from entering the United States, a national security directive with enormous externalities. Politics dominate the relationship between the United States and China, and dominate my understanding of China. The Communist Party dominates China. At its top, General Secretary's Xi Jinping's grip over the army, the People, the Party, and the nation appears viselike. China is annexing parts of Bhutan, harrying the Philippines and threatening Taiwan. War between the United States and China looms.

From the United States today, Six Records feels like a reminder of both the China that flourishes at a distance from the politics – and that China could have gone down a different path. China did not need to evolve into a one-party dictatorship. The Party positions itself as the apogee of history. But one day it will be gone, like ripples on a still lake. I remind myself of the obvious but overlooked difference between the Party and the people it rules, and I feel sorrow for how history has evolved into a dangerous present. The 2020s won't be remembered as the decade Chinese or American people got to enjoy "the little pleasures of life" or of "the joys of travel." Even Shen's record of "trying sorrow" feels quaint, his problems and his aperture small and manageable.

---

112. Here I must apologize for quoting myself, with permission: America Second (Knopf, 2022)

If a Chinese Pierre Menard were to write Six Records today, I'd read it as a plea for placidity. "In a China with a quickly growing economy," Six Records responds "to the psychological needs of Chinese people eager to escape the pressures of life and work," a Chinese professor wrote in 2023.[113]

Yes, existence contains struggle. But "death and life are governed by fate. Let's not worry needlessly," Shen writes. Why mire oneself in spiraling thought patterns about an intense work culture, the trauma from COVID prisons, or if one's only son may die storming the shores of Taiwan? Let's not, a Chinese Pierre Menard would say. Break from gazing inward, into that churning of your mind. Gaze instead outward, to the "fishing boats scattered like stars on the tranquil expanse." Gaze instead upward, to the heavens.

"The moonlight was beautiful that night. Down in the river we saw ripples shimmer like silver chains. Dressed in light silk garments and with small fans in our hands, we sat side by side before the window overlooking the water. Above us, we saw clouds flying across the sky, transforming into myriad shapes.

'All the vastness of the universe shares this one same moon,' Yun said, 'I wonder if there are others in the world who are in a similar mood to ours tonight.'"

Isaac Stone Fish
June 2025

---

113. https://www.chinawriter.com.cn/n1/2023/0131/c419384-32614804.html

First Readers

Zachary Hayworth (2) USA
Hope Laurie Kurens (1) USA
Nick Bruce (1) USA
Johannes Scheuer (1) USA
Zhigang Fang & Weijuan Ma (2) China
Chong Gu (3) USA
Fanhao Yang (1) USA
Yasaman Moghadamnia (1) USA
Pierre Amiel (1) USA
Sebastien Smith (1) Taiwan
Ellis Marte (1) USA
Kyle Skinner (1) USA
Xiaoxi Zhong (1) USA
Jia Can Xu (1) England
Yichen Lu (2) England
Simon Preker (1) Germany
Jinwen Fu (1) USA
Sharon Liu (1) USA
Yuhan Lu (1) China

Lucy Williams (1) England
David Zhang (1) USA
Kaley Mi (1) England
Brice Green (1) USA
Carly Yang (1) Canada
Vincent Lan (2) Netherlands
Heather Zhou (1) USA
Jasmine Teng (1) USA
Linh Nguyen (1) USA
Ali Tehrani (1) USA
Marie Patino (1) USA
Beverly Kogut (1) USA
Xinmiao Liu (1) USA
Heather Colley (1) England
Brian Zielenski (1) Taiwan
Peter Knych (1) USA
Saaman Moghadam (1) USA
Laura Shao (2) Hong Kong
Jiahong Zheng (1) China